LET iT HAPPEN!! :)

VISION
MINDSET
GRIT

How to Stand Up When Life Paralyzes You!

SCOTT BURROWS

**PEARHOUSE
PRESS**
.COM

Published by Pearhouse Press, Inc., Pittsburgh, PA 15208
www.pearhousepress.com

First Printing: January 2013
Second Printing: September 2018

Printed in the United States of America

ISBN: 978-0-98867-210-9
LCCN: 2012922184

Cover and Book Design: Mike Murray

TABLE OF CONTENTS

*This book is dedicated to the people who have
inspired and mentored me not simply to
survive, but to live and flourish before, during
and after my life-changing accident — those
related and close to me, others distant, some
famous and still others relatively unknown,
but especially the audience attendees who
have heard me speak around the world. They
motivate me to continue sharing my message
of hope, and they never fail to inspire me.*

FOREWORD

VISION, MINDSET AND GRIT** will not tell you how to earn a million dollars, add 30 pounds of muscle or win the Nobel Peace Prize. There are no false promises. If you are prepared to put aside any notions you may have, this book will take you on a journey well worth the ride.

My son, Scott Burrows, has had to fight his entire life—in ways most people fortunately never have to contemplate—to arrive at where he is today. He has faced many challenges in his life, both personally and professionally, but none as severe as lying on his back paralyzed from the chest down and diagnosed a quadriplegic.

Along the way, he has learned how tough obstacles can be and the importance of being ready for the next and the next and the next. As Scott says, "Tough battles continue to happen in my life, and I am guessing you face a never-ending series of battles as well. Maybe most of yours have never been on the scale of the worst of mine, or maybe you have been through worse." We each operate from our own unique perspective, and the obstacles we face can loom large. It is Scott's hope you find this book to be a useful tool that will help you leave your paralyzed state, metaphorically speaking, finish a task, complete a job and move on to what is next with a renewed sense of vigor, purpose and accomplishment.

Throughout the book, Scott draws upon three words: **Vision,** **Mindset** and **Grit.** As he employs them, **Vision** refers to the goals and aspirations you have for yourself, your family, your career and those around you. Your *Vision* is the ending point to challenges and barriers you will encounter along the way as you strive to achieve higher ground. *Mindset* refers to the continual mental orientation and preparation needed to meet oncoming challenges and help you get to where you want to go. *Grit* is the day-to-day determination to persevere when you are otherwise too tired, too sore or too beleaguered to continue on. Having *Grit* means drawing from within to move forward when all else beckons you to retreat, fall back, give up or, perhaps worst of all, simply stay where you are.

Scott offers insights and perspectives that can help readers turn more of their dreams and their personal and professional goals into realities. By figuratively putting you in his shoes, inviting you into his life and taking you on what has proved to be an incredible journey, you will be able to look at your own life's challenges from a new perspective. Having a better understanding of the *Vision, Mindset and Grit* principles, you will be armed with the tools and techniques to guide you to higher ground.

All you have to do is *let it happen!*

— Tom Burrows, Proud Father

INTRODUCTION

My life, like my body, has taken many twists and turns over the last quarter century. As a result of my trials, tribulations, successes and failures, my family encouraged me to share my story with the world in the hope that it will inspire others to never give up regardless of circumstances.

I wrote this book with the help of others to inspire and motivate people to take action. I wanted to help other people learn from my experience so they could become stronger and stand up to any challenge that might come their way. I wanted to encourage people to reach for new, exciting opportunities and grip onto them tightly, while letting go of paralyzing fears preventing them from living their lives to the fullest.

Each chapter has a special section focusing on *Vision, Mindset* and *Grit* to help you apply these principles in your own life so that you may overcome obstacles and "Get a Grip" when things seem to be spinning out of control.

As you read through this book, I challenge you to reflect on your own life—how far you have come, the choices you have made and the challenges you still are trying to overcome. I encourage you to use the strategies I suggest, because I believe they will help you become stronger and more capable of standing up to anything that comes your way. With this knowledge, I know you will experience life more fully and freely heading well into the 21st century and beyond.

— *Scott Burrows, Motivational Keynote Speaker*

July 1984: My last kickboxing fight, broadcast on ESPN, at the West Palm Beach Florida Auditorium. I won a unanimous decision.

CHAPTER 1

IN THE BLINK OF AN EYE

On the morning of November 3, 1984, I awoke having no idea that before the day's end everything about my life would change catastrophically in mere seconds. I was just 19 years old, on top of the world and believed I was invincible. One year before, I had made the Florida State University (FSU) Seminoles football team as a walk-on wide receiver. I also was ranked #1 in the State of Florida's Light Heavyweight Kickboxing Division, having had my most recent fight at the 5,000-seat West Palm Beach Auditorium broadcast on ESPN. I was dating my high school sweetheart and had been selected by my college peers to appear as "Mr. September" in the Men of FSU calendar. Most importantly, I had a wonderful, loving family and the best friends of my lifetime.

In Mere Seconds...

In the handful of defining days of your life, personally or professionally, certain details have a tendency to become etched in stone, don't they? That particular Friday afternoon in Tallahassee, Florida, was beautifully sunny with temperatures in the mid-70s and crystal-clear blue skies. After class, I spent much of that afternoon playing coed pickup basketball with friends. Then, in our characteristic spontaneous nature, we decided to go on a quick getaway weekend to the gorgeous, white sand beaches along the Gulf of Mexico. Our excursion from FSU began around 6:30 p.m. We loaded our gear into the car and began the 90-minute drive south to a stretch of beach on pristine St. George Island.

We arrived around 8:00 p.m. just as the moon was rising above the eastern horizon. We set up camp, built a fire and nestled around it for hours on end telling story after story with our best teenage, hormonal sense of humor. That's when a friend, Ed, challenged me to an impromptu foot race. Being just a little competitive, like you, I welcomed the challenge by taking off my tennis shoes, bending down and leaning forward into my running stance waiting to hear "Go." Imagine hearing that word echoing through the air, and within seconds all you can feel is the cool night air blowing through your hair. With each step you feel sand gritting between your toes and, as you cross that imaginary finish line, you can even taste the salt in the ocean air. It turned out to be one of my best runs ever, and at that moment I did not realize it would be my last.

Once we caught our breath, we walked back to camp, where another friend asked Ed and me if we would take a ride down the beach to find more firewood to keep our bonfire burning through the night. We willingly agreed. I jumped into the passenger side of Ed's car and off we went. Finding some firewood, we headed back to the campsite.

In 1984, the drinking age in Florida was 21. We were underage and had started drinking when we arrived at the beach. To top it off, seat belt usage was not mandatory in the state, and I foolishly had not been wearing mine

On our way back, speeding along on a dark, lonely road, Ed lost control of the wheel and veered sharply. He was able to recover and get us back into our own lane. "Are you okay?" I asked. "Put your seat belt on if it's not on," he yelled, but before

I could check, he lost control again and the car once more veered off the road.

Ed tried to recover a second time, but as he was making his way back onto the surface we hit a mound of sand, projecting the car into the air in ski-jump fashion. It nosed over and fell back to earth, then tumbled end over end. In that brief instant, now frozen in my mind forever, I sensed there would be an impending, horrific outcome. For a split second, I could see our headlights shining in the sand. "Oh my God," I cried out, "we're rolling!" A fraction of a second later, I was unconscious.

Unknown to us at the time, two other friends, Scott Sears and Charles Benoit, had also gone on a firewood scavenger hunt and witnessed everything. They came upon our accident and found me still seated in an upright position in the passenger's seat, with blood running from the top of my head down my face and onto my clothes.

Miraculously, Ed had not been seriously injured and exited the car to help Scott and Charles rescue me.

Dark Road, Dark Times

No one knew I had broken my neck or sustained a very serious spinal cord injury. Their hearts were focused on getting me to emergency care immediately. There were no homes, hotels or stores close by to call for an ambulance and, of course, back then no one had a cell or smartphone to call, text or tweet for help. As carefully as they could, my friends extracted me from Ed's car and transferred me into their vehicle.

They drove back to camp. The news spread like wildfire. Friends like Dee Dee Hicks and others decided to follow Charles and Scott to the closest hospital, George E. Weems Memorial, 50 miles away. I recall waking up once. I was sitting up in the back seat, contorted, my head and torso facing slightly to the left and my legs pointed 45 degrees to the right. I had intense neck pain and tasted iron—blood was running down my face into the corner of my mouth. I could not move my legs and had no control over my hands or fingers. In my state of half-consciousness, I was groping for answers, trying to get a grip on the situation.

It seemed the strength I had from my shoulders allowed me to twist my body back and forth. When I twisted, my legs did not respond. In the back seat on a pitch-black night, speeding down a lonely road, with friends desperately transporting me to a hospital, I grasped my worst nightmare. I yelled out, "Oh my God, I'm paralyzed!" Within moments, I blacked out.

Immobile and Unconscious

When we arrived at the emergency entrance of Weems Memorial Hospital, I was unconscious. My friends lifted me out of the car, carried me in to the building, set me down in a chair in the waiting area and frantically sought assistance. I was later told I woke up briefly complaining of neck pain. Hospital staff scurried in with great urgency. Before being X-rayed, they stitched up an eight-inch laceration on the top of my head. The X-rays confirmed I had broken my neck. Weems Memorial did not have the facilities for my type of injury, so they quickly secured me on a gurney and transferred me into an ambulance to be rushed to Bay Medical Community Hospital in Panama City, Florida, 100 miles away.

After arriving at Bay Medical, I awoke on the emergency room table with a special team of doctors standing over me. In a whirlwind, my favorite college fraternity T-shirt and pair of blue jeans were cut off with scissors. As my clothes were removed, I could see they were covered in blood. Then I was asked all kinds of questions: "Son, can you move your arms? How about your legs? Can you feel us touching your toes?" Each time, my answer was either "No" or "I'm not too sure."

A Terrible Nightmare

Minutes passed, but seemed like hours. I was terrified. I wished I could close my eyes and wake up from the nightmare. Then, without warning, I felt the most excruciating sharp pain coming from both sides of my head, close to my temples. It felt as though my head was caving in, as if someone was crushing it in a giant vise.

What I did not realize was that my doctors were placing me in spinal traction, Gardner-Wells tongs. It was performed by screwing two metal bolts, stainless steel screws a quarter of an inch in diameter, into my skull to stabilize my neck while attaching 40 pounds of weight to hold it securely in place. The pain was unbearable and I screamed at the top of my lungs, pleading for it to stop. As my vision dimmed, I remember thinking *This is it—I'm going to die!* All I could do was pray and hope I would survive as I slipped back into dark unconsciousness.

The Nightmare Continues

Around 2:00 a.m., my parents received the most unimaginable phone call that left them paralyzed in their tracks. Dr. Stringer, my neurosurgeon, told them what had happened and announced my grim diagnosis. He said, "Your son was involved in a serious automobile accident. He is currently stable and in intensive care. He broke the cervical sixth and seventh vertebrae in his neck and has sustained a severe spinal cord injury, leaving him paralyzed from the chest down and diagnosed a quadriplegic."

On November 5, 1984, at Bay Medical Community Hospital, during my parents' first visit, Dr. Stringer said he was going to perform cervical spine surgery. The surgery would involve removing bone fragments from my neck and then taking one of my rib bones from my lower back left rib cage and fusing it to my neck. The justification for surgery, described in my doctor's notes, was as follows:

> *Various risks, possible complications; operation will not help recovery of neurological function. Primary for stabilization of cervical spine. Also, possibility of further neurological injury which may occur either during surgery or thereafter.*

From that point forward, my dad felt compelled to begin chronicling the entire ordeal through diary posts and Kodak

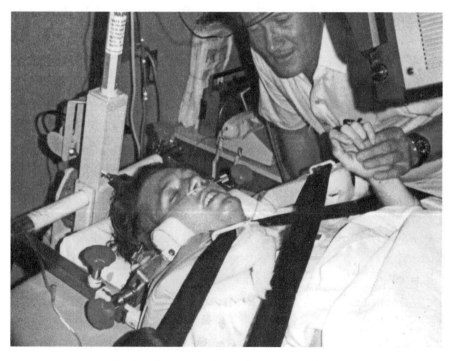

Dad and me two days after my accident.

pictures. After the first day, my mom, Joan, took a picture of him leaning over me and holding my hand. That day he wrote in his notes, "Joan and I are almost at the point of collapse."

When I was fully awake several days later, Dr. Stringer walked into my room, introduced himself and gave me the grim news. He said, "Scott, you may or may not recall, but you were involved in a serious car accident a few days ago. You have a broken neck and sustained a severe spinal cord injury, leaving you paralyzed from the chest down and diagnosed a quadriplegic." It was not long thereafter I was told I would never stand, walk or run again and that I might be dependent upon family, friends and caregivers for the rest of my life. At that moment I thought, "How do you go from having the time of your life to being told that if you are going to survive and make the best of your new situation, you need to start dreaming new dreams and setting new goals?"

In seconds, all of my plans and dreams were hijacked by the ordeal of simply trying to stay alive. I was terrified. My body was now a public spectacle. I had no privacy. Water, sustenance, basic bodily functions—all were out of my control and handled by strangers. In spite of my new set of circumstances, I remember feeling blessed to be alive. I am a Christian and believe, even to this day, that things happen for a reason.

I was strapped to a rotary bed designed to move very slowly from one side to the other to prevent bedsores and pneumonia. If not turned while on your back for a period of time, your heels, tailbone and shoulder blades do not receive adequate blood circulation, causing your skin, tissue and muscle to break down. Unfortunately, over the coming weeks, bedsores developed on both of my heels, eventually exposing bone. Those open sores did not heal for an entire year.

Tight stockings were placed on both of my legs to prevent blood clots, which are all too common among quadriplegics. As the days passed, a steady parade of doctors and nurses came and went 24/7. They continually checked the intravenous tubes, slated more X-rays, marked their charts and injected me with pain medications and steroids to reduce the swelling in my neck. Swelling, one of the biggest problems with spinal cord injuries, can crush the spinal column and lead to complications beyond the initial injury.

Mind Games

Over the first week, I was medicated to the hilt and began to hallucinate in vivid detail—always the same two dreams. I would wake up in the middle of the night, unstrap myself from the rotary bed, unscrew the steel bolts in my head, sneak out of the hospital, run back to my college apartment for a good night's rest and set my alarm for 4:30 a.m. so I could return to the hospital, sneak back into my room, strap myself back into the rotary bed and screw the bolts back into my head before my nurses realized I had gotten away; or I would be in a room with a bunch of people in wheelchairs, would climb out of my wheelchair, begin to walk and then start running. Then I would wake up!

It is mind-boggling how one moment life can be so grand and seconds later it can all collapse in a shattered dream. As I lay there, I was gripped by the terrible realization of how little I was capable of doing now. If the side of my face itched, I could not scratch it. I would have to lie there with a tormenting itch or ask someone to scratch it for me. As I struggled with my emotions and my mind's games, my doctors could not tell me what I desperately needed to know: *Will I ever stand, walk or run again? What are my odds?* I had so many questions, but the replies were always the same: "We don't know."

Just Let It Happen

My doctors didn't have any answers, and I spent day after day lying in my hospital bed in excruciating pain consumed with fear, not knowing what the future held. At my lowest moment, my father did something that gave me hope and put me back on the road to recovery. When we first saw each other, he brought me a golf club. Knowing I had a tremendous passion for the game, he gave me the club so I would have something to shoot for. Then he said, "Son, if you can, *let it happen*." With this simple act, my dad was telling me to be patient and that by not resisting the experience, I would get through it even though it would take time.

Over the coming weeks, I started coming to terms with my father's words, but the truth is it's easier said than done. I realized I could not change the past, no matter how hard I tried, and go back to the way things were, so I had to carve out a new life for myself as different as it may be. I began to understand what had happened to me and that I must make the best of it. I decided I wouldn't fight it, but that I would do my best to embrace my dad's words that now were giving me the strength, drive and willingness to persevere with grit and determination.

My dad was teaching me something he had learned in an EST seminar: "Do not resist what is happening to you right now, but embrace it. Do not expend unnecessary energy fighting what it is; make space for it." EST (Erhard Seminars Training), an organization founded by Werner H. Erhard, teaches people "To transform one's ability to experience living so that the situations one had been trying to change or had been putting up with clear up just in the process of life itself."

Life – It Is What You Make of It

I know you may never experience a situation as transforming as what I've just described, and I'd never wish that upon you or anyone else, but I do know you have your own life and business challenges, challenges you are trying to navigate, conquer and learn from, as well as your own fears, doubts and uncertainties. In that sense, perhaps you and I share something in common. Whether your life has been turned upside down or your dreams have all been shattered, I am telling you that you can prevail, but you must want it in ways you've never wanted anything before.

Things never looked as bleak for me as they did so many years ago in the hospital with steel screws in my head and nurses taking care of all my most personal needs. I had lost an active life full of over-the-top experiences and had descended to the valley of the shadow of death. Yet, with his actions and words, my father had inspired me to look toward the future, to try to grasp onto what I still had and to use it to rebuild my life.

During that difficult time, I started believing that we can always choose to dream again, to live again and to move forward with a positive attitude and a high degree of optimism regardless of circumstances. We can choose to set goals that stretch the mind. We can choose to believe that the most overwhelming setbacks can be converted to success, fulfillment and personal realization. We can choose to believe there are no barriers or stop signs, just detours and workarounds. We can also choose to inspire. What I never could have envisioned in my wildest dreams was how the simple act of gripping a golf club, listening to my father's words and not giving up on my faith would motivate me to work extremely hard to recover from my life-threatening injuries and go on to live a new life.

VISION

Vision refers to the goals and aspirations you have
for yourself, your team, your organization, your
career and those around you and your family.
Vision is the beginning point to the challenges and
barriers you will encounter along the way as you
strive to stand up and achieve higher ground.

● ● ● ●

MINDSET

Mindset is the continual mental orientation,
preparation and actionable adjustment needed to
meet oncoming challenges and changes. It's your
Mindset that creates a winning attitude, spurs you
on to take action and helps you focus on what you
can control, especially when you feel your Vision
will no longer become your reality.

● ● ● ●

GRIT

Grit is the day-to-day determination to persevere,
to be resilient in your pursuit when things around
you begin to spin out of control or when you are
otherwise too tired, too sore or too beleaguered
to continue. Having Grit means drawing from
within to lean forward when all else beckons
you to retreat, fall back, give in or, perhaps
worst of all, simply stay where you are.

CHAPTER 2

A NEW NORMAL

From that first day to several weeks after the accident, I kept replaying the sequence of events leading up to the accident, as if by analyzing the situation I could change the reality. My mind was bombarded with questions I could not answer. We were 10 weeks into the semester by that fateful day. It was a pleasant afternoon. The beach trip was spur of the moment. What if I had not gone? What if I had simply stayed in Tallahassee?

Our destination was St. George Island, and the drive would take about 90 minutes, so we wouldn't arrive until after dark. Why did I agree to seek out firewood? Why did I choose not to wear my seat belt?

Anyone who goes through an unplanned and irrevocable life-changing event will most likely ask these types of questions. You try to relive in your mind all the choices you made leading up to the catastrophic event to find a way you could have made another choice or done something differently to erase that split-second moment so that everything could become normal again.

What You Can Control

Of course, that is a mind game, and that mindset was leading me nowhere. I had to change my thinking. I quickly learned that to sustain positive thinking, you must be willing to stop focusing on what you cannot control in life, such as:

- I was now novocain numb from my shoulders all the way down to the ends of my toes.
- My body was now a public spectacle; I had no privacy.
- Worst of all, no one could tell me what I desperately wanted to know: "Would I ever stand up again on my own? Will I walk or run again? What are my chances?" The replies were always the same: "We don't know."

I thought about my future. Would I be able to finish college? Would I ever work? Would I ever get married and have kids? Would I have any quality of life? Would I be able to play sports? Would I struggle to take care of myself and be dependent on caregivers and my family for the rest of my life?

If you have ever experienced a radically life-changing event, you understand what I was going through. However, at some time in our lives, most of us experience difficulties that throw us into turmoil. Maybe you are trying to make financial ends meet, planning for a college education or a wedding, having a difficult time in your relationship, struggling to overcome career roadblocks or taking care of aging parents. Perhaps you are trying to get promoted at work or hit new benchmarks, or maybe you are trying to distance yourself in a super-competitive industry. Your challenges may have flared up suddenly or have been building slowly. Whatever they are—at home, at work, in sports—I have learned you can't always change what is, but you can change how you think about it. And that will change what is to be.

Stretch Beyond Limitations

An important person who helped me cope with challenges and ease my fears after the accident was my physical therapist, Leslie, a 5-foot-5, reddish blond full of energy. She loved calling Physical Therapy PT. I called it Pain and Torture! Leslie loved stretching me out. She enjoyed pushing me and helping me move beyond my own self-perceived, paralyzing limitations. During our time together, she told me, as had my doctors, that no two quadriplegics are the same. The extent of the paralysis depends largely upon where you break your neck and how badly you damage your spinal cord. If the spinal cord is completely cut, similar to that of the late Christopher Reeve, it cannot be put back together even with today's technology. However, if the spinal cord is damaged, there is an outside opportunity that the brain might be able to communicate with some of the paralyzed muscles. There is no guarantee, but some return of movement in your arms, hands or fingers can make the difference in being able to take care of yourself or being dependent upon others for the rest of your life.

Leslie was an important person in my recovery because she gave me inspiration and hope. She told me there was a chance I might get some return of movement back in my arms because it happens to most quadriplegics. She said if that happened, then she and my occupational therapist, Karen, and the recreational therapists could teach me how to drive again. Can you imagine having that kind of freedom back in your life? Just the thought of being able to drive a friend, a customer or business associate out to lunch or to a weekend ballgame. How about finally having access to all those reserved spots! "Rock star" parking has definitely been an attention-grabbing change in my life.

The Knee-Jerk Reaction

Speaking of change, our world continues to change at the fastest rate in human history. Today we have social media such as Facebook, Twitter, Instagram, Snapchat and LinkedIn as well as other emerging technologies, and we also have the undying need for speed. I need it and I need it now! It is amazing to see how fast we can communicate with each other and send and receive information in a moment's notice by texting.

It was not too long ago people were suggesting that if the speed of technology continues to impact our lives at this rate, we will have a tremendous amount of free time! I am curious, how are you enjoying all that free time that technology has introduced in your life? If you have a smartphone, Android, iPhone or a tablet, ask yourself how much extra time you have. If anything, technology has made our lives busier.

Focus on Positives

The one thing I learned about change is that resisting it is futile. We cannot change the past, and our futures are not guaranteed, but we have today. We have the power to choose how to respond to life, our world and a business environment that refuses to stay the same. Change begins by opening your mind to new possibilities, new ideas and new solutions.

I responded to the paralyzing changes in my life by focusing on the positives as opposed to dwelling on the obvious and overwhelming negatives. This focus created a clarity that helped me articulate multiple visions, such as what it would be like to run again, get dressed or simply take a bath on my own. Although most of my nurses were really cute, every now and then one would walk in at 6-foot-5—and he would weigh 250 pounds.

I visualized everything because it was all I could do, but I made a point while lying there to go with change. I wanted to

19

make a positive response to a life that refused to stay the same. I was determined to push forward in the only way I could through my Vision.

What motivates you to keep pushing forward into your future regardless of circumstances? Think about that for a moment, then ask yourself: What is my Vision? What are my short- and long-term goals? What am I fighting for in my personal and professional life, metaphorically speaking?

I knew what I was fighting for when I entered the kickboxing ring a few months before being paralyzed from my chest down and diagnosed a quadriplegic. I wanted to win. Ironically, I knocked my opponent out 42 seconds into the first round, which was a stretched goal, but I knew all along what I was fighting for. What are you fighting for right now? What do you want to achieve? What does that look like in your mind's eye?

The tough part is turning your Vision—those things you are fighting for—into your new reality. It's hard to transform your ideas, your creativity and innovation, and the goals you want to achieve in your personal and professional life into reality. Life rarely happens in a straight line; often it moves forward in fits and starts with unexpected changes. For me, my new Vision, walking again, came to a complete stop in one 45-day period of time.

Complications Galore

Ten days after I broke my neck I developed a fever that spiked to 103 degrees, followed by a bladder infection. Mucus had built up in my lungs, leading to a severe case of pneumonia, and three days later I simply lost my breath when my right lung collapsed. I was placed on a respirator to control my sporadic breathing, and my weight plummeted daily. I dropped from 180 pounds to just under 140 pounds in less than 45 days, and that was without the help of Jenny Craig!

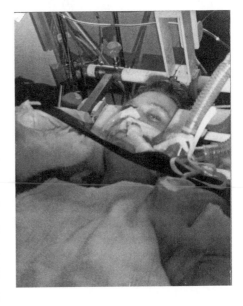

It seemed impossible to recover as each new day posed another major concern. Perhaps you know that feeling, or maybe you are experiencing it right now. You might not like all the challenges standing in front of you at home in your finances, with the kids or in your professional life, but you are the only one who can rise to those challenges and overcome them. Perhaps these include basic operational and support difficulties at work or trying to establish a successful culture and foundation with limited bench support. Depending upon your personal and business challenges, you might ask, "Do I even have the strength within to stand up to the challenges facing me?"

That was the question I was asking myself, and all I could think about were those things over which I had no control, such as being confined to a wheelchair and cared for by others. I know you can identify with your own physical limitations: your work load, the cost of groceries and gas, what's being broadcast over the news 24/7, government intervention and regulations, a fluctuating stock market, taxes, the weather, the next move your competition will make and so on. However, I have learned by using the concepts of Vision, Mindset and Grit that it is possible to focus more on those things you can control, like being willing to learn from your mistakes, being honest with yourself, being patient, setting priorities, having integrity, making a contribution to society, maintaining a strong work ethic, keeping the lines of communication open with your family and friends, delegating responsibility, learning from trends, goal planning, building trust and, most importantly, being unwilling to give up.

What I have learned and want to share with you is that by focusing on what you can control, as opposed to obsessing on those things you cannot change, you can and will go on not only to achieve your goals successfully but to exceed all expectations.

It's Murderball Out There

Speaking of expectations brings me to the subject of Wheelchair Rugby or, as it is affectionately known, Murderball, a full-contact, Paralympic sport played by athletes who:

- Have extreme weakness in all four extremities
- Amputation in four extremities
- Neurological impairment in four limbs
- Physical impairments in four limbs to include hands and/or feet
- A combination of any of the above

To play this sport, athletes must retain the ability to push a manual wheelchair on their own. Murderball is played in "Mad Max–style" wheelchairs on steroids custom designed to take full contact hits. These specialty wheelchairs cost upward of $4,000 and, unfortunately, are uninsurable.

Wheelchair Rugby combines elements of basketball, handball and ice hockey. The object is to carry a ball across an opponent's goal line with at least two wheels of the chair crossing the line. The sport was started in Canada as an alternative to wheelchair basketball, which is difficult for people with diminished arm, hand and finger capabilities to play.

The best way to see what I am talking about is to watch a clip on YouTube. Try Googling Wheelchair Rugby or Murderball or rent the documentary film *Murderball*, featuring two guys I know, Mark Zupan and Joe Soares. If you do, I'm sure the first question you would ask is, "Scott, aren't you afraid you will break your neck again?" A typical rugby response would be, "I already broke my neck once. How bad could it get?"

I have a great deal of passion for the sport because it gave me an opportunity to compete with some of the best physically challenged athletes from all over the world—Australia, New Zealand, Japan, Canada, Germany, Great Britain and many more. People like us come together as a team with the goal of continuously stretching our Vision and ensuring that our mindsets do not become our biggest handicap. It is this type of thinking that will bring out the champion in you.

I had been extremely active before my accident, and one of the most devastating thoughts I had to overcome was that I would no longer be able to compete, since I had limited arm strength and no hand or finger strength at the time. It seemed it would be that way for the rest of my life. Fortunately, within a month of being injured, I began to regain some strength in my arms, hands and a few of my fingers. That is when I started focusing on what I could now control physically. I found a new Vision, and, in time, David Gould, a friend of mine and another quadriplegic, introduced me to Murderball. That sport helped me to exceed some of my physical expectations, and I learned that when things in life start spinning out of control, it is possible to change your thinking and focus on what you can control.

Giving Back to Humanity

I want to fast-forward to January 2012 for a moment and share an experience that caught me totally off guard and humbled me at the same time. I was the keynote speaker for Scott & Stringfellow's, a federally registered investment advisor in Richmond, Virginia. There were 250-plus top-producing financial advisors attending their annual conference. After my kickoff presentation, a gentleman by the name

Rugby: Me between two defenders.

of Adair walked over to me. He said, "I was very moved and impressed with your talk and would like to donate $10,000 to any organization that has great meaning to you." Adair wrote a check to the 2012 USA Paralympic Quad Rugby Team.

The letter below came from the Lakeshore Foundation in Birmingham, Alabama, where the 2012 U.S. Paralympic Wheelchair Rugby Team was selected during a training camp. Twelve players and three alternates were nominated to the squad that competed in the 2012 Paralympic Games in London that began August 29, 2012. The U.S. team was both the defending world and Paralympic champions in Wheelchair Rugby, having defeated Australia for gold at both the 2010 World Championships in Great Britain and the Beijing 2008 Paralympic Games.

"The team we selected, from top to bottom, is a great example of the very best the United States has to offer," said head coach James Gumbert. "Our expectations are to play to the highest level of rugby possible. The U.S. has a high standard, and it's this team's desire to improve and play above the standards set before us."

About the competition the team will face, Gumbert said, "We are very excited to be able to compete on the international stage again, and we respect our opponents and look forward to playing against them." Gumbert said the team's motto, *Together as One*, will be the phrase that leads the team to London.

Wheelchair Rugby was one of 21 sports featured at the London 2012 Paralympic Games, August 29–September 9, 2012. More than 4,200 athletes from 165 countries faced off in London at the largest Paralympic Games to date as the event returned to its birthplace in England. Team USA went on to earn a Bronze medal. The act of giving back to humanity has changed my life and has inspired others like Adair. Imagine what it could do for you.

In the face of circumstances that are out of our control, life that has changed radically, and any situation in which you find yourself that you cannot change, I am telling you to make the decision to change your thinking and *let it happen*. Focus on those things you can control, then stand up to your challenges, get a grip on your actions, do what it takes to make it happen and get ready for the ride of your life!

V I S I O N

Vision in a champion is composed of several elements. One element is mental toughness. Champions know that our thoughts can be controlled. We can harbor negative, self-defeating, time-wasting thoughts, or we can choose to envision new goals for ourselves. Set new goals today and focus on them, not on the "If onlys."

• • • •

M I N D S E T

Mindset supports Vision by constantly bringing your mind back to what your Vision is. Once you have determined your new Vision, then your Mindset will be one of continual focus on that Vision. Your greatest tool in life is your ability to focus. Use that ability to create a Mindset that is focused on your Vision.

• • • •

G R I T

Grit is the practical application of Vision and Mindset. When circumstances are beyond your control, when life has taken a sudden turn, and you begin to change your Vision and realign your Mindset, you will use Grit day after day to focus on where you are going, not where you have been. It takes Grit to stick with a new Vision, Grit to keep your mind from straying and Grit to engage in the new activities that will be generated from your new Vision and Mindset.

CHAPTER 3

LAUGHTER IS THE BEST MEDICINE

In Christopher Reeve's autobiography, *Still Me,* he wrote how he had received a visit in the hospital after he broke his neck falling from a horse. When his good friend Robin Williams, the comedian, stopped by to cheer him up, he came disguised as a doctor zealously announcing he was a proctologist. He then put Reeve through a routine about having to look up his derriere until Reeve finally figured out who he was. At that point, Reeve could not help but laugh and said that until Robin Williams' visit, the hospital room had been so somber he could not stand it.

I, too, learned that the power of laughter can be our saving grace!

Within a few days of my accident, college friends came to visit. They did a decent job of lightening things up. I was sleeping, strapped down in my rotary bed moving slowly from one side to the other. My friends John Salvador, Brendon McCarthy, Hank Dobbs, Steve Muro, Bill Haas, Sunni Kittrell, Dwight Gorall and others with their teenage sense of humor, along with my girlfriend, Kristin Carpenter, sneaked into my room and mounted pictures of Suzanne Somers, the famous *Three's Company* actress who had recently been featured in *Playboy* magazine, on the ceiling above my bed. When I woke up and took notice, all I could do was laugh. So did my parents, my friends, my doctors and the nursing staff. When the news broke out, unexpected visitors, people we didn't even know, showed up to have a look!

Sweet Sensations

Today, I am still numb from my chest down as a result of my spinal cord injury, and the doctors tell me it will be this way for the rest of my life. It is a tingling feeling, like being injected with novocain all over the body. However, since I had feeling, even though it was not how I used to feel, it was a positive sign that my spinal cord had not been severed. It meant that some messages from my brain were reconnecting to the lower parts of my body.

Speaking of reconnecting feelings, two years after I left the hospital I began to experience chest pains and checked myself into the emergency room. It was crowded, maybe 20 people were waiting, and I didn't know how long they had been there. When the nurse who was collecting my personal and insurance information asked me what was wrong, I told her I was experiencing chest pains.

She then asked if I had done anything different or outside my normal routine in the last 24 hours and said whatever I told her would be confidential. I said, "Yes," became embarrassed and told her I had been with my girlfriend the night before. We had gone out to dinner, caught a movie and afterward we had talked and listened to music. One thing had led to another. We had a romantic experience I thought I might never have again after being paralyzed from the chest down and diagnosed a quadriplegic. All of a sudden, the nurse said, "That's amazing." Then she leaned forward and gave me a high five!

She then sent me immediately into the emergency room. I said, "What about all those people in the waiting room who have been waiting for hours to see the doctor?" She replied,

"There is no waiting for anyone who comes in experiencing chest pains."

I was hooked up to an EKG machine. Tests were run. In the meantime, my room was like a revolving door, with a steady stream of nurses coming and going, emergency room doctors and injured patients stopping by to say, "Congratulations!"

So much for doctor-patient confidentiality.

Fortunately, all the tests came back negative. My doctor determined that my pains were the result of hormones my system had not seen in two years and told me the chest pain was actually a good sign and I should expect them to subside. She said, "Have fun and keep up the good work!"

Laughter from Afar

In 2008 I was invited to speak at a conference for ICICI Prudential in Agra, India, famous as the site of the Taj Mahal. On the flight over the Atlantic, I read about Dr. Madan Kataria in Mumbai, who had come across a study of the health benefits of laughter. That study examined how laughter can reduce stress, anxiety and depression. It also revealed how laughter can redirect your thoughts if you are overwhelmed and can lead to increased productivity.

That doctor was so inspired that he started a laughing club. He went to a local park to recruit people who were exercising early one morning. Only a few people were interested in joining his club, but Dr. Kataria was undaunted and, armed with jokes, he had everyone laughing for more than 30 minutes. They had so much fun that by the end of the week the news had spread and over 50 people were now attending. That is when the doctor ran into a brick wall: he ran out of jokes. Being quick on his feet, he realized he could still get people to laugh by making faces, grunting or telling short stories.

Interestingly, that doctor from India closed his medical practice in 2001 and launched Laughter Yoga International. To date, there are more than 16,000 Laughter Yoga clubs in India and 6,000 more across 60 countries. Dr. Kataria's innovative concept has been widely accepted all over the world and has been written about in prestigious publications such as *Time Magazine, National Geographic, The Wall Street Journal* and many others.

"We now have laboratory evidence that mirthful laughter stimulates most of the major physiologic systems of the body," states Dr. William Fry of Stanford University. Dr. Fry, an expert on humor and health, says that a good belly laugh speeds up the heart rate, improves blood circulation and works muscles all over the body. "It's an aerobic exercise and, after the laughter is over, you feel relaxed," he says. Laughing heartily for a period of 10 minutes can equal 15 to 20 minutes on a treadmill.

Gang Tackled

I remember the time I entertained the entire FSU football team during a college football scrimmage. I was the punt returner. A few seconds after the ball was punted, I was about to catch it, then I glanced down the field to see if any running lanes were open. At that moment, three unblocked guys were about to gang tackle me, so I panicked, waved my hand back and forth and yelled over and over, "Fair catch, fair catch." Our head coach, Bobby Bowden, then screamed, "Burrows, you idiot, we said no fair catch in the scrimmage. Catch the ball, son, catch the ball!"

Bam! I was laid out by three people! By being classified an idiot and not paying attention to instructions, I had everyone in tears and rolling in laughter. Yes, me too!

Undoubtedly, you have your own set of challenges. Maybe you are dealing with a troubled teen, or perhaps you are navigating your way through the pieces of a failed project or trying to find the time to accommodate a difficult customer. Maybe you are trying to become a world-class organization as you face growing pains in the start-up phase. Conceivably, some of you may be trying to contend with operational and support challenges as you strive to be first in your industry while establishing a winning culture and foundation with limited bench support.

Whatever your challenges are, one of the most significant and helpful things you can do is to take time to laugh. Take a moment away from the seriousness of your life and just laugh. When Dr. Norman Cousins, the well-known American political journalist, author, professor and world peace advocate, was diagnosed with a severe arthritic condition that was not relieved by pain medication, he taught himself to laugh by watching Marx Brothers movies. He said, "I made the joyous discovery that ten minutes of genuine belly laughter had an anesthetic effect and would give me at least two hours of pain-free sleep."

I learned the benefits of laughter at a young age and know you will, too!

VISION

A new Vision is sometimes hard to grasp
when you are overwhelmed by circumstances and
difficulty in your life. Take a few moments today
to laugh. Find a comedic movie that you like, a
sitcom on TV or a book of jokes. Engage in good
belly laughter. You will relieve your stress, and
the result will be a clearer mind and an ability
to see the future with hope.

● ● ● ●

MINDSET

Create a Mindset that encourages laughter. Look
for the humor in life. As your Mindset changes
and you seek the funny moments, you will find
yourself becoming more creative, more responsive
and more interactive with life and with others. You
will, before you know it, start to have a Mindset
that is focused on the positive things.

● ● ● ●

GRIT

Grit will help you with your new Vision and
Mindset when circumstances bear down on you
and once again everything seems to be spinning
out of control. Use Grit to go to the store and buy
a book that makes you laugh, or rent a video.
Call a friend who makes you feel better.
Remember all the benefits of humor and continue
to use them in your life to seek the positive, lighter
side. Laughter and happiness are two different
things. You don't have to be happy to laugh,
but laughing can make you feel happy.

CHAPTER 4

VISION

We all have Vision, even if we have not taken the time to articulate it. Vision is founded in our belief system and, in part, determines how we respond to our circumstances. Those responses lead to the important choices in life, like taking an optimistic approach to your dreams, your setbacks, your difficulties, or a positive view of your short- and long-term goals, your hopes and aspirations.

Vision is Personal

When you proceed in life with a proactive, positive Vision, you serve as the locus of control in your life. You can have a Vision for many aspects of your life—extracurricular activities, college, career, relationships, finances, sports, spirituality, customer service, sales, business and so forth.

Vision Spurs Us to Action or Inaction

Vision doesn't apply to just the extraordinary moments in life or to the newsmakers. Do you know someone who gets up every day and goes through the same routine, doing the same kinds of things in the same ways? That person is acting out his or her Vision just as surely as someone else who has a grand Vision and makes it come true.

Vision without imagination tightly bound is based on what has already happened and on the belief that there is nothing better to attain. However, Vision with imagination can bring you everything. I found that when the Vision of life that was rock solid and sure to happen has been stripped away, we still can rethink new possibilities and create a new Vision that will inspire us to keep pushing forward.

When we create our Vision, we are empowered to stretch beyond our comfort zone and bring that Vision to life. When we just move through life with no Vision, our lives have no course of action, no direction and no goal. Take time now, this moment, and start to create a compelling Vision that you are passionate about. Where do you see yourself in six months, one year or five years from now? What do you want to accomplish beyond the success you already may have had? How about taking a risk and stretching to turn an impossible goal into reality?

Poise and Execution

I met John Schmitt in Athens, Greece, in 2008 after a conference. Schmitt was the center for the New York Jets in the late 1960s. He played in the 1969 Super Bowl III against the Baltimore Colts, one of the most notable games in history. The New York Jets were deep, deep underdogs. Joe Namath, their cocky and overconfident quarterback out of the University of Alabama, predicted victory. The media buildup before the game was unprecedented.

Over dinner, John got down on one knee and told me that Weeb Ewbank, the Jets' head coach, would preach two words to the team every day. Those words were *poise* and *execution*. Ewbank told the team that if everyone was on the same page both on and off the field, if they kept their poise on the field and didn't panic, especially when the pressure was on during the game, they'd go on to do what everyone was predicting they wouldn't do—win a Super Bowl Championship.

Ewbank imprinted those words, *poise* and *execution*, on the minds of every player on that team. He created a Vision of players who would maintain their *poise* and *execution* through the most difficult parts of the game, be *poised* to take advantage of every opportunity and be ready to *execute* the maneuvers needed to win. In that moment, John's eyes turned red and filled with tears. He took off his monster-sized Super Bowl III Championship ring and put it in my hand. With great feeling, he carefully detailed how the team reached the Super Bowl and won it. He told me that day, more than three decades later, the entire team had bought into what the coach envisioned and had preached all season.

There is a lesson here for all of us. Poise will see us through even in those moments when the pressure is on. If we maintain our poise, don't panic and execute the moves we have practiced, then we, like the Jets in Super Bowl III, will prevail. Moreover, when we imprint our Vision firmly in our mind, we will be able to *execute* it with *poise*.

The Art of Visualization

My experiences before, during and after my life-changing accident have helped me understand the importance of Vision. I'd like to share with you some of the techniques that have helped me with Vision, because I believe they will help you as well.

I was born in Highland Park, a small town in Illinois just north of Chicago. At age five, my family moved to Lake Geneva, Wisconsin, when my dad received a job offer he could not refuse: golf course superintendent of the Playboy Club owned by Hugh Hefner. He got me involved in sports right away. Dad took me to work with him on Saturdays, too, and I will never forget the first time he put a golf club in my hand and taught me how to grip it.

Our Playboy-sponsored baseball team. I was 7 years old at the time—
#6 is me (third boy from left, standing). My dad is the tall guy, far left.

I have been in love with the game ever since. From that moment, he began teaching me the art of visualization. He planted a seed in my mind when he told me that to have a competitive edge you must see your golf shot in your mind's eye *before* you execute your swing. Whether the shot is two feet, 20 yards or 180 yards away, Dad said, "You'll be more successful hitting the ball and having it land where you want if you first picture it in your mind." That is not to say that a player cannot step up to the ball, simply swing correctly and knock it down the fairway, but for most players that simply doesn't happen.

I believe the edge is with the person who uses Vision before every stroke. You have to see the shot, step up, aim and swing. My dad repeated it over and over. To me, it seemed like endless repetition in my mind when I was on the driving range. What I didn't realize at that young age was the inherent strength in visualization.

We use visualization all the time without even knowing it. Visualization is just a thought with a picture applied to it. So, if you need to go to the store, you see yourself getting up, grabbing your coat and keys, getting into your car and driving to the store. This visualization happens very quickly and we don't even realize it has happened.

We can make use of this powerful, natural tool to experience more success in our lives. A lot of elite athletes like Lindsey Vonn, Jack Nicklaus, Kerri Walsh and Arnold Schwarzenegger as well as successful people like actor Jim Carrey, Amazon founder Jeff Bezos and Oprah Winfrey use this powerful tool. Take the Vision you have developed and begin to actually see it in your mind's eye. If you have a Vision for a better career, give it life and depth in your mind. If you are envisioning a stronger body in better shape, picture that every waking moment. What are you fighting for? Vision costs nothing, but it can bring you everything. By picturing your Vision, you are learning to focus on what you can control.

You can't always choose the precise outcomes of the choices you make in your life. When I started school at FSU, I had a completely different Vision than the new one I had to develop after November 3, 1984. When your outcome doesn't meet your dreams, remember that you can always create a new Vision, and then focus on that as often as possible every day.

Imprinting

The next time you approach a key personal or business struggle or opportunity, I challenge you to use a technique I call "imprinting." It is a technique I learned from my days of playing college football. Imprinting in this sense is seeing complete success in your mind's eye first. See yourself conquering a challenge or reaching a goal, an aggressive goal. Visualize it, then repeat or imprint that successful outcome over and over again. When you imprint the image so frequently that your subconscious mind can no longer tell the difference between your heavily etched idea and what is real, your Vision becomes reality.

By imprinting your challenge, your Vision, those things you are fighting for, into your subconscious mind, you develop a

Mindset designed to do everything within its power to achieve whatever you tell it. This anticipatory approach can put you in a position to overcome your challenges, reach your goals and turn your ideas into reality. Imprinting helps to maintain your Vision in spite of change and ongoing challenges. Remember, the brain believes what you tell it, so always strive to be positive.

Regarding imprinting, I am reminded of my Golden Retriever, Codi. Early in her life, Codi became imprinted on the soles of my shoes and experienced complete success every time she tore through another pair. That imprinting became her reality. Never be afraid to imprint your idea into your subconscious mind!

Dreaming in Full Color

Roger von Oeck, author of *A Whack on the Side of the Head* and *A Kick in the Seat of the Pants*, said it best when he wrote, "It is easier to tone down a wild idea than it is to tone up a bland one." Or a boring one. What he is saying is that we need to dream big, to visualize with gusto, to go for the gold. So, the way I see it, we need to be dreaming in Full Color in all areas of our lives, and we need to keep doing it until our Vision becomes our reality. We can always tone down our dreams later.

What would you like to see in your life? What can you do to expand that Vision, those things you are fighting for, to make it bigger and better? What do you really, deep down, want in life? Create and explore unlimited Vision—like Steve Jobs, Steve Wozniak and Ronald Wayne did when they founded Apple Computer on April 1, 1976—and then take time to develop your Mindset on how you will achieve it. If your mind can see it, believe in your mind and heart that you can achieve it, especially if you are willing to persevere and be resolute.

I was inspired by the outlook of Michelle Wie who, at the age of 15, declared herself a professional golfer, signed $10 million in endorsement contracts and competed against the best male golfers in the world. Her outlook was one of a big, Full Color Vision. I believe the same outlook can be equally as inspiring in the business world. The founder and chief executive officer of Starbucks, Howard Schultz, had a Vision that a premium cup of coffee delivered in a warm and relaxing environment would bring a premium price. He was dreaming in Full Color. He was creating change, as opposed to sitting down and waiting for change to happen. He was doing what his competition was not willing to do, and his Vision led to extraordinary success. The same goes for actress Sofia Vergara, who co-founded Latin World Entertainment, a talent-management and entertainment-marketing firm, as well as Arianna Huffington, founder of *The Huffington Post*, after selling her company to AOL for $315 million. Arianna said, "We need to accept that we won't always make the right decision, that we'll screw up royally sometimes—understanding that failure is not the opposite of success, it's part of the success."

Challenge yourself to stay away from the boring ideas that you may have to tone up. Go with the wild ideas; you can always tone them down. Start with a Vision of *all* you can achieve. See it in Full Color and then believe you can achieve it.

Think big; add color and life to your Vision!

Breaking Out of Self-Perceived Limitations

In our super-competitive world, if we are not stretching, acquiring, developing and practicing new skills and following our passion, it is likely we are dwelling within our comfort zone—a place I refer to as a paralyzed state. The problem arises when we linger there so long that our comfort zone becomes a place of refuge and we are afraid to leave.

If we are going to grow, we must stretch ourselves beyond our comfort zone. When we do this, we may experience uncertainty, discomfort, change and possibly even chaos; however, it is only when we learn to open ourselves to new ideas that we can expand our possibilities. Speaking of expanding possibilities, what can we learn from Elon Musk? He's a business tycoon, investor and engineer and the founder, CEO and lead designer of Space X, and the co-founder, CEO and product architect of Tesla, Inc. Elon continues to stretch himself, experiences uncertainty, learns from his mistakes and is open to new ideas. In doing so, he is changing the world.

When we are expanding, we are learning; when we are learning, we are growing; when we are growing, our Vision, Mindset and Grit strengthen. For this reason alone, we need to try something completely out of the ordinary—to do things differently than we ever have before. If you are a customer service representative, a manager, a nurse or a front-line employee, strive to take a leadership role. If you are in inside or outside sales, be open to looking at your book of business from a different point of view. If you are an executive, a president or a CEO, try coming to work as one of your own employees to see your business from their perspective. If you are in college and want to improve your grade point average, try emulating the success of a peer making A's. If my examples do not resonate, take a moment to question how you can do something differently in your life.

An Enemy to Our Vision

I believe our comfort zone is the enemy that prevents us from realizing our dreams, goals, hopes and aspirations. When complacency rules, we are doing more harm than good. Think about it for a moment. How can we excel if we always operate within the confines of our paralyzed state?

Ask yourself at work, when you are in your paralyzed state, if you are serving your customers and their best interests. Don't some solutions require us to stretch our thinking? Maintaining the status quo is fraught with danger, and complacency drives mediocrity. What industry is safe from the constant arrival of advancing technologies and new forms of competition? That is why it is so vital to flex our risk-taking muscles and break out of our comfort zone. It isn't always necessary to take physical risks, but it is imperative that we open our minds to new ideas and are willing to take more meaningful, calculated and informed risks to improve our lives.

Who among us can risk simply staying put? Times are changing at the fastest rate in human history, and the rate of change in our lives is accelerating beyond measure. Today, if we are not stretching, blending new cultures, embracing diversity and inclusion, challenging our thinking and sharing common values, we are likely falling behind. If you just stand still, chances are you will be passed.

The go-getters in life seem more willing to embrace the ever-increasing speed of constant change. They may not like it, but they understand that change is reality and that they must embrace it to welcome new possibilities. The go-getters take a creative value approach to what they can profitably offer the world and go after it by educating and reeducating themselves on ways to improve. They know that thinking more creatively leads to higher productivity.

Create a Captivating Vision

Realistically, the pace of change in our society will not stop accelerating. Even if you are sitting at home on your derriere in your favorite chair watching TV, you cannot avoid change. Ultra high-definition TVs are here, but they, most likely, will be replaced in the future. If you are not suitably equipped, you will be facing a blank screen. Even as a consumer, you will find it necessary to keep pace with what is available.

When is the last time you enrolled in a course to become more technologically proficient? In today's world, your ability to think creatively or innovate and your willingness to try new and different approaches to challenges now dictates the quality of your life, both professionally and personally. Your ability to understand and cope with new technologies can be significant in realizing your Vision.

The quest for balance in life is more important than ever before. To attain a sense of balance and peace of mind, you must carve out the time and space for it as an integrated part of your Vision. To live a fulfilling life, we need to recognize the value of proper sleep, nutrition, exercise and intellectual stimulation, as well as spiritual growth. Most of us will live many more years than we currently presume. Life is not a sprint; it is a marathon. Does your Vision entail planning to actively participate the whole way through in the marathon of your life? Are you preparing now for the 10, 20 or maybe even 30 extra years you may live?

If you think you *cannot*, then surely you *will not*. Each of us must continually assess what is important in our lives and what is not. Our ability to stretch and set our sights on a new Vision gives us an opportunity to experience life at a different level. Remember, your goals are uniquely yours. They can be large or small, short- or long-term, for your career or your entire life. Other people might see your dreams as grandiose, unreachable or even inconsequential, but who are they to judge? Your dreams belong to you. Create a captivating Vision, one that entices you to take action, to succeed!

"You gain strength, courage and confidence by every experience in which you really stop to look fear in the face. You are able to say to

*yourself, I lived through this horror. I can take the next thing that
comes along. You must do the thing you think you cannot do."*
— *Eleanor Roosevelt*

⤚

V I S I O N

Explore unlimited Vision of what your life can be. It costs
nothing at all to see with your mind's eye. Spend time today
envisioning all that you hope to accomplish. Find what feels
right for you—no one else's dreams will be right for you.
Create your own Vision for your own life. Once you begin,
your ability to see will become stronger with practice.

● ● ● ●

M I N D S E T

Your Mindset will help you imprint your Vision.
Utilize Mindset to allow your Vision to become fully
realized. Put detail to your Vision and learn how to dream
in full Technicolor. This imprinting in Technicolor will
energize your Vision and increase the reality for your
subconscious mind, which is working 24 / 7 on your behalf.

● ● ● ●

G R I T

It takes Grit to see beyond our self-perceived limitations.
Like starting to work out in a new exercise routine
or discipline, it can be somewhat painful to stretch
your thinking. Your Grit will help you continue to focus
on breaking free, learning and growing. With Grit,
you will leave your paralyzed, complacent state of
mind behind and allow your Vision to flourish.

CHAPTER 5

MINDSET

Anything is Possible

Once you know your Vision and what you are fighting for, you have a new beginning. When you can see your Vision clearly, you can overcome tremendous odds, achieve overwhelming results and break new ground while establishing a winning culture. Recondition your Mindset to put yourself in a better position to turn your Vision into reality.

Between the ages of 8 and 19, I had the opportunity to study martial arts. During this time, I earned my first degree black belt in Pai Lum Kung Fu, competed in numerous karate tournaments around Florida and Georgia and was fortunate to have had my last kickboxing fight broadcast by ESPN.

The martial arts teach you to never lose the ability to be a student—always asking, always seeking. A student of education, your industry, your craft. A student of leadership, team building, personal and professional growth and so on. The martial arts also encourage you to ask, "What don't I know? What am I missing? What can I practice next?" *What* questions also open your mind to seeing life and your challenges from an entirely different perspective, which can help you problem solve.

Competing at the age of 10 (in black).
My first karate instructor, Royal West, is at far right.

Royal West, my first karate instructor and one of my early mentors, once said in a newsletter, "The reason so many people fail to achieve the impossible in their lives is because they view it [the impossible] as an excuse to not discipline themselves to take some sort of action." Bruce Lee said, "Knowing is not enough, we must APPLY. Willing is not enough, we must DO."

If you knew you could achieve the seemingly impossible or reach a difficult goal, ask yourself, "How would I be willing to approach my life differently tomorrow, personally and professionally? What would I be willing to do tomorrow that my competition is unwilling to do?" I'd encourage you to use your imagination, to think in Full Color. These types of questions help you recondition your Mindset to believe that anything is possible and that impossibilities can be turned into possibilities.

Unshakable Belief

I have learned that strengthening Mindset begins with an unshakable belief in the person you are on the inside when no one else is around. Mindset is what you believe about yourself, your abilities and skills. It is your willingness to keep pushing forward with a positive attitude, especially when you feel your Vision will no longer become your reality.

Lying on my back, paralyzed from my chest down, I came to believe that if I listened to my dad and stopped resisting the experience and embraced it while keeping my faith, then maybe I would not only survive, but perhaps I could beat the odds and turn my impossible dream of standing and walking again into reality.

I was dreaming big and in Full Color, but the truth is I have always dreamed big. It started at a young age in sports. Winning meant the world to me. It was the high of all highs. The passion to chase dreams and the adrenaline rush of winning in sports and in life motivated me to stretch above and beyond the expected. I was not a superstar athlete. I had to fight every inch and stand up to my competition, but I believed I could give them a run for their money.

One of those things I had always wanted to do, but never did while growing up in Florida, was to learn to scuba dive and spearfish. Now, if I wanted to learn to do those things in my paralyzed state, I would need to change my Mindset. I would need to get out of the Mindset of being cared for 24/7 by my nurses and into the Mindset of doing something different. I would need to go with what scared me. Remember, I had a collapsed lung—not a good thing if you are looking to scuba dive.

So what is Mindset? It is the conscious and continual mental orientation, preparation and adjustment needed to meet oncoming challenges. In a sense, it is what you do with what you can control. There are so many things in our lives we wish we could change. My question to you is, "What are you going to do about it, and what *can* you do about it?" From my perspective, you can choose how you look at things, how you interpret them and how you react to them. That's Mindset. Your Mindset will change your outcome, or it will keep you stuck deep within your comfort zone.

Make a Plan and Act on It

One thing you can control is making a plan and then acting on it. Nothing exemplifies this more than Amazon. One of the largest online retail websites in the world continues to expand through acquisitions. Some companies you may recognize are Zappos, Double Helix Games, Avalon Books and Whole Foods Market. I've found that the best plans are helped by a positive attitude and a proactive outlook. Develop the habit of initiating action as opposed to letting things happen to you, especially when you are attempting to achieve something unprecedented in your personal history. Patience is a virtue, but too often the potential you have can dissipate while you wait for fortune to smile upon you.

I've heard it said that there is genius in boldness. Taking action is often better than doing nothing. At least you are making waves. Once you are in motion, if you make an error, you can adjust with a course correction. If you are not taking action, there is nothing to adjust, but there is also no forward progress. Just like riding a bicycle, you must grip the handlebars and pedal to create motion and then you can learn to control that motion. Without the motion, nothing happens—the bike just falls over!

Go With What Scares You

The actress Helen Hunt inspired me with her Mindset. She started acting at age 10 in a weekly TV show and later moved on to movies, such as *Cast Away* with Tom Hanks, *What Women Want* with Mel Gibson and *Twister* with Bill Paxton. At age 35, she won the Oscar for her role as a single mother and waitress grappling with the idea of having Jack Nicholson's character as her lover in *As Good As It Gets*. After winning the movie industry's highest accolade, she was asked, "Now that you have won the Oscar, we hear you are receiving a number of different types of movie scripts to choose from. How will you go about choosing the role that best suits you?" Hunt said, "I'll go with what scares me!" Think about that statement for a moment and ask yourself, "What kind of Mindset do I need to go with what scares me?"

Interestingly, as I was putting the finishing touches on this book, Hunt was starring in a new movie, *The Sessions*, in which she plays a professional sex surrogate. The movie is based on a true story about Mark O'Brien, the real life poet-journalist who spends most of his day confined to an iron lung. Permanently disabled after contracting polio as a child, Mark cannot move from the neck down. He does feel sensations, however, and when he turns 38 he is determined to lose his virginity. That's where Hunt comes in. I think it's serendipitous that this movie about paralysis came out when it did (as I was writing about my own paralysis) and that Hunt, pursuing what scared her (being naked on screen, for one thing), is generating Oscar buzz once again.

From my perspective, our comfort zone, our paralyzed state, could use a little shaking up. Sometimes it's necessary to be scared and take a calculated chance; it helps us overcome inertia and get out of our paralyzed state. It was that kind of Mindset that led me to believe if I *let it happen* and stood up to my fears that I could overcome them. You know the fears I am talking about. We all have them. Mine was the fear of never walking again. That's probably not your fear, but every fear, large or small, can have a paralyzing effect on us. By going with what scares me, embracing my fears, I began to see them as stepping stones I could cross one at a time. If something seems to be a huge leap for you, then that is the issue you may need to tackle first to embrace and conquer your fears. If you approach the task you are most afraid of before any other, it will no longer be a hindrance. What kinds of fears are holding you back today?

> *"Courage is doing what you're afraid to do.*
> *There can be no courage unless you're scared."*
> — *Eddie Rickenbacker*

Fear of Commitment

To commit to something means to turn away from other things and focus on the task at hand. Sporadically diverting your time, energy and focus across the board leads to low productivity and little satisfaction. For so many people, attention seems to be diverted in every direction other than where it's most needed. If it has been a long time since you've summoned your powers of commitment, it might mean that you need to develop new habits to stay ahead of the curve.

The problem is we live in a world of immediate gratification. If we can't have it now, we move on. Nothing is more emblematic of this phenomenon than the internet. When seekers of information visit a website and explore for a few seconds to find a cooking recipe, sport highlights or other information, but don't quickly find the answers, they move on to another site with the click of a mouse. The information they were looking for may have been there, but if it was not readily available and directly in the forefront to see, the website lost their interest.

It is also easy to engage in behaviors that are temporarily satisfying, but ultimately unrewarding. However, the professional who comes to work to win practices what Dr. Aubrey Daniels calls the "Grandma Principle." In his book *Bringing Out the Best in People*, Daniels stresses the importance of scheduling a reward following a good performance. As Grandma would say, "You cannot eat your ice cream until you eat your spinach!" Then there's the famous Pink Floyd lyric: "How can you have any pudding if you don't eat your meat?" If you are facing an unpleasant task, it makes sense to follow up with something you enjoy doing, instead of the other way around. Eat your meat, eat your spinach and finish with the ice cream and pudding!

Fear of Taking a Different Approach

Making a change in how we have always done something can seem threatening. Yet, much of what worked yesterday is going to require some flexibility to be more effective today. There are a handful of times that golfing legends such as Phil Mickelson and other top male and female golfers have changed their golf swing when they were performing at their best. Media outlets, sports pundits and other golfers frowned on the idea. However, these professionals were taking a risk to try something different in their approach to see if they could perform even better. In most cases, they continued to excel.

When I was lying in my hospital bed, I tried something different. I changed my Mindset from asking the *Why* questions about my new set of circumstances to asking the *What* questions. This was a significant adjustment I will talk about later.

Sometimes we hang on to our settled ways simply because we have been doing them that way for so long we would never consider the possibility of changing our approach. When we try a change that does not work, we revert to our old ways out of sheer comfort. Researchers tell us as we continue to perform the same behavior in the same way, we develop strong neural pathways in the brain. What you did before becomes the path of least resistance. It is easy to keep doing what you have been doing. This is not to say we cannot change, but the longer we have been doing something, the more inclined we are to keep doing it.

Fortunately, other studies indicate that human beings have the capacity for substantial change even at advanced ages. Whereas once it was thought that language skills, music abilities or certain types of expertise could not be acquired by the elderly, we now know that as long as you are alive and your mind is fully functioning, you can learn new skills, take a different approach and make things work by just making a commitment to yourself, your family, your team and your company. As we continue to repeat the new ways, our minds adjust and accept them as the standard, and then the new way becomes our habit.

One of the most important times to use Mindset is when you have experienced a radical change in your life. When it seems like all your dreams are shattered and lay in pieces at your feet, when your business is facing closure, when your company is laying off workers, when rapid changes in technology seem overwhelming, that is when you need to flex and strengthen your Mindset and use it to control what you can. A strong Mindset will help you overcome the fear of commitment and the fear of taking a different approach.

Mindset is the one thing you can control completely. Like Helen Hunt, like golfers who change their swing, like Olympic athletes who change their starting foot, you also can go with a new plan of action, even if it scares you. Keep your Mindset flexible and use it to change your outcome.

VISION

Find the passion to pursue your next level of achievement.

• • • •

MINDSET

Stay true to your goals and business plan in this ever-changing marketplace; adjust your vision as circumstances change.

• • • •

GRIT

Make it a habit.

CHAPTER 6

GRIT DETERMINATION

Grit determination is a powerful tool that involves personal discipline, belief and the willingness to persevere while being resilient in the pursuit of your long- and short-term goals. When you know your Vision, what you are fighting for and have developed the Mindset of how to turn that Vision into reality, you will run into barriers. As I mentioned, life rarely travels in a straight line. When you veer off course by your own doing or when facing unforeseen obstacles, grit determination will help you overcome challenges and be successful. With perseverance and grit determination, you will believe that adversity and change can become opportunities, and you will achieve positive outcomes.

Speaking of grit determination, a few weeks after I was injured, my beautiful grandma, Alpha Winters, traveled from New York to visit me. I knew she was devastated, but she did not show it. She encouraged the family to have faith, and she encouraged me to keep fighting, to never give up hope and never give up on God. She and my mom were an inspiration. They both sat by my side and helped me so much during that trying time in my life. They made me feel comfortable, cheerful and loved. The healing power of love and support from others is irreplaceable, mentally and physically.

When I think of grit determination, I often ask myself why only a small fraction of people who set out to accomplish their Vision have the Grit to persevere, to discipline themselves to see it all the way through. We all know people who are visionaries, who have wonderful ideas, dreams and aspirations. They may even have the Mindset of a winner to proceed toward it, but for some reason they give up too soon.

I have found it is vitally important to believe in yourself, to be self-disciplined and to persevere if you want to accomplish your goals despite difficult circumstances. I've been told I have a strong sense of self-confidence, but I know I wasn't born with it. I believe my self-confidence began the day my dad handed me a golf club at an early age and encouraged me to learn to play the game. My dad believed in me. He thought I could be a good golfer and I believed him. Remember what I said: your brain believes what you tell it.

My dad is a great golfer. He turned down scholarships from a number of schools because he really wanted to attend Penn State. No scholarship was available there, however, so he paid for his own education just so he could go there.

It is important to learn new things because that is how we grow. I believe from the bottom of my heart that we all can learn something new each and every day to improve our lives. If you are open to learning and looking at your business and life challenges from a different perspective, you will try new approaches and you will reach successful solutions. Trying something new and succeeding builds confidence.

The "One-Thirds"

Over the years, I have learned that all of us have good intentions. We want to reach above and beyond the everyday and achieve extraordinary results, but for some reason often things do not work out that way. I have come to believe:

- One-third of us will challenge ourselves. We will give it a shot, but not our all, and if we do not see immediate results, we will simply give up.
- One-third of us will challenge ourselves. We will even go the extra mile, but as soon as we are tried and tested more than once, we will throw in the towel.
- One-third of us will challenge ourselves to persevere, to be resilient in our pursuit—this day, this week, this month, this quarter—knowing that nothing worth achieving comes easily. We will not give up until we achieve our goal, what we are fighting for. This is Tremendous Grit in action.

Grit is as much a habit as is failing. It's also a noun and made up of hustle and passion. You must develop the Mindset to believe in the near impossible and summon the Grit to grind it out if you want to conquer challenges and meet your expectations in spite of adverse circumstances.

Winning the Inner Game

A small percentage of people persevere to achieve what they want to have in life. You can slow them down, but you can't stop them. Take a look at Travis Kalanick, who built Uber Technologies Inc., which is a peer-to-peer ride sharing, taxicab, food delivery and transportation network company. Today, Uber is an industry disrupter and one of the most feared and valuable start-ups on the planet. But the road has not been easy. Uber has fought regulators, rivals, threats from the taxi industry and competition from around the world. These people know that you can have the most highly concentrated Vision and the Mindset of a world champion, but they have learned that neither of these two elements will be truly effective unless combined with the discipline and perseverance necessary to see things through. That takes Grit.

Giving something your all yields an inner sense of satisfaction that is hard to describe. After Spanish tennis star Rafael Nadal played and lost a grueling five-set match, an interviewer wanted to know how he felt. Nadal said that when he is on the court he gives everything he has. He cannot play any harder than he does. When the match is over, he has no regrets.

What a brilliant response. Whether he won or lost the match, he had no mental regrets about it because he had approached the match with as much Grit as he could possibly summon. I have heard people talk about "Giving it your all" or "Offering 110 percent," but I have never heard anyone link having Grit to investing all their emotion in the task. Because Nadal *gave everything* during the match, he was content despite the outcome.

Beyond the Tedium

Having Grit means putting in the time and effort to do the little things, over and over, as tedious as they may appear. If it supports your Vision, you must be willing to launch head-on into doing repetitive or even tedious jobs, because these daily tasks contribute to your overall progress and help you realize your goal.

Unexpected Results

I will never forget the morning Leslie walked into my room. I was smiling ear to ear. She said, "I am glad to see you are in a great mood." I said, "Check this out. Watch my right wrist." Then I focused like I never had before, and my right wrist moved about one-eighth of an inch. I know that doesn't seem like much, but to me it was as if I had just moved a mountain. Leslie congratulated me and said, "Now my team and your occupational therapist, Karen, can teach you how to use your hands without the independent use of your fingers!" I said, "It sounds great to me, but they don't work," but like any teacher, mentor or leader, Leslie showed me the way. She told me that if I was willing to be more flexible than ever before, I could change the outcome and the direction of my life.

To understand what I mean, I want to share something with you. Hold your arm straight out in front of you and relax your wrist completely. Notice that your hand and fingers are in the down position. Now, do you see the gap between your index finger and thumb? From that position, keeping your fingers very relaxed, curl your fingertips in slightly and extend your wrist up as far as it will go. Keep it in that upright position for a moment. Notice how your index finger and thumb automatically come closer together, if not touching?

Now, drop your wrist so your hand and fingers are again in the down position. Notice how your index finger and thumb automatically separate. Now, bring your wrist up again to where your index finger and thumb come closer together. When your fingers come together, that is called a "tenodesis" grasp.

By being more flexible than ever before and focusing on what I could physically control—with lots of practice, repetitively moving my wrist back and forth, over and over again, with the goal of strengthening them—I eventually learned how to pick up a straw, a pencil and a plastic fork using only my index finger and thumb. This was a major accomplishment! And, I finally understood why Karen, my occupational therapist, kept calling occupational therapy OT. OT stands for Overtime, the driving force behind reaping what you sow.

After I perfected this technique, something occurred to me. When I saw my mom, my brother, Mark, and my sister, Heidi, for the first time, I was unable to embrace them. At the time, my arms didn't function well, but when my wrist was in the down position, creating that gap between my index finger and thumb, I could do something I never thought I'd do again: shake my father's hand! It is such a simple gesture and one you may do frequently throughout the week, but on that day, that human connection had profound impact and meaning for me: I started believing that no matter how difficult the road would be, everything was going to be okay!

As I share that experience with audiences around the world, what keeps me going is the feedback. Recently, Mike Norman, the director of human resources for a major apparel company, asked me to address their front-line employees. Mike saw me speak at a management conference, and his team felt their front-liners should hear my story. It took place at their distribution facilities in Atlanta and North Carolina. Those facilities are open five days a week, 24/7, and they have three shifts. To make it work, I spoke twice at two different times at both locations. When I returned home, I received an email from Mike that touched my heart. Mike said, "You connected with people. And from my perspective, you certainly helped us attain our goal of challenging and inspiring our associates to be the best they could be every day...I hope that I get to meet your dad someday. I would like to shake his hand and thank him for encouraging you and for not letting you become defeated. I pray that God will continue using you as an inspiration to others. Let me sum it up this way. If I ever have the opportunity to listen again for the **sixth (6th) time, I will be in the front row!"**

Your Ability to Grip

My ability to Grip onto something was a huge turning point in my life. I knew it would have been easier to just give up on the therapy. The repetitions to strengthen my wrists were endless and the results incremental at best, but I persevered because I wanted the end result. I wanted to achieve my Vision, so I was willing to repeat the same task over and over, to use Grit to get the result I was shooting for.

You have to understand—I love life—always have, always will, regardless of circumstances. I might add that it's sometimes easier said than done. Lying on my back, I came to believe that if I listened to Leslie and my team of therapists, I would prevail, have a good quality of life and, ultimately, become independent. My Grip was my strength. Yes, the far-stretched goal I was fighting for was to walk again. It is good to start by aiming big. Will you hit that mark? Maybe, maybe not, but if you put forth a strong effort and give it your all, then you already will have gone a long way toward building confidence. Learn to believe in yourself. We all are capable of so much more. Once you have overcome the fear of taking action, you will have gained the confidence to continue moving forward, and eventually you will succeed.

Once you accomplish your goal—something you are fighting for—you will have the confidence to continue to turn your dreams into reality. I achieved a few major goals in my life in sports, but I also failed many times. However, every time I failed to reach a goal, I kept an open mind and learned from the experience, and you should, too. This type of thinking builds confidence, and that confidence puts you in a much better situation to prevail. If you believe in yourself and learn from your experiences, you will begin to see things in a different light.

Having been diagnosed a quadriplegic, I had to work hard to achieve the smallest things, starting with my Grip. My goal was to become stronger. I had small and large goals. Yes, the big one was to walk again, but I was told that goal might be impossible to achieve. Nevertheless, I refused to give up. I was determined to prove my doctors were wrong. I had proven people wrong in the past. I was told I would never be able to compete in a top-ranked football program, but I did. I was told and led to believe that only highly recognized people, famous people, could succeed at becoming motivational speakers. I did not buy into that type of thinking and, as a result, have traveled the world as an inspirational speaker and presented to Fortune 500 companies using my life-changing story to help others believe in their innate power to succeed.

In your own life, many tasks may appear to be tedious. Take a moment and think about some of them. What are a few of those things you do daily that might be considered mind-numbing? When you are just going through the motions or in that repetitive mode doing the same things over and over again, daily and weekly, and when you would rather procrastinate or are seriously considering giving up, that is when you need to get a Grip and use your Grit as the top "one-third" people do.

Grit is a key ingredient to peak performance.

Grip, Applied and Released

When you spend as much time as I did strengthening my hand and fingers, you begin to view them differently. From a metaphorical point of view, our hand might represent a family or an organization, and our fingers could represent the people who make up that entity. As you look at your hand and begin to wiggle your fingers, you will notice they are all independent of each other. They can move in the same or different direction, but they still are connected to your hand. Similarly, you are connected to your family or your organization.

Now, reach out and Grip onto this book, a pencil or the person sitting next to you. What just transpired? You made a point to come together as opposed to remaining independent. That is teamwork, and that's where there is strength in your Grip, as well as the Grip of a team. As we come together, I am reminded of the quote from Aristotle, the Greek philosopher, who said, "The whole is greater than the sum of its parts." Acting alone, each part brings limited value to what you are attempting to accomplish, but acting as a well-managed, coordinated team, the combined value is far greater than the sum of its parts. Coming together gives you the advantage and puts you in a better position to tap into the minds of others to help meet and accomplish dreams, goals and objectives. When I present to organizations, I often use the metaphor of the hand and fingers to encourage people to work together as part of a team. After a recent presentation, Mark Bruner with J4 Communications, on behalf of Robroy Industries, wrote, "Scott was able to link individual achievement with the role of an individual helping a forward-thinking team to become more than the sum of its parts." I am so gratified when I receive such positive feedback, because I know my message has been heard and has made a difference in the lives of many people.

In the weeks following my accident, my biceps and right triceps began to fire back to life. Not fully, I might add, but something was better than nothing. It was an amazing feeling. As my team of therapists helped me strengthen them, my Grip was also getting a little stronger. Two months into therapy, I practiced and eventually relearned how to dress myself in under an hour, and how to push and stop a wheelchair. My Grip and my Grit created unexpected opportunities, and I know your Grip and your Grit will do the same.

Get a Grip

The first time I learned about Grip was at age 5 when my dad was teaching me how to play golf back in Wisconsin. I practiced my Grip over and over, visualizing the results all along the way. Grip was also significant to me in football when I joined the FSU football team as a walk-on wide receiver. Wide receivers must have a powerful Grip—they are sought out for their ability to hang on to the ball under any and all circumstances.

Grip is also important in all aspects of life. Grip gives you control. By Gripping your Vision, your hopes and dreams, your Mindset will help you go where you want to in life. If you are not exercising your Grip in life, you will just slide along, moving indiscriminately and without direction, never exercising control over where you are going. Without Grip, your energy, your concepts and your ideas will never be shared and your dreams never fulfilled.

When you have Grip, you know who you are and where you are going. Relaxing your Grip allows you to let go when a situation has gone beyond your control. Those who struggle to relax their Grip find it difficult to make forward progress. Their rigid Grip on life keeps them stuck in place, unable to grow personally or professionally or even to see that change is necessary.

A tight and controlling Grip on a golf club will cut off the energy in your swing. Gripping a football with no flexibility in your arms may cause the ball to "squirt out" the moment you are tackled. A tight, clamped-down, rock-hard Grip in your life may bring little progress and much frustration. Your Grip must be strong enough to weather the storm, but flexible enough to know when the wind has changed and you need to go in another direction. When we go in a different direction, we will need to persevere and put our Grit into action to see results.

True Grit

The stories of people throughout history who have used their Grit can be especially inspiring. When Germany invaded Poland in September 1939, Great Britain entered World War II and took on the Nazi war machine with little international support for what must have seemed like an eternity to the inhabitants of that island. It was another 27 months before the United States entered the war and joined Great Britain in the fight for their lives.

Winston Churchill, Prime Minister of England during World War II, gave one of his most quoted speeches in the House of Commons on June 4, 1940:

> *Even though large tracts of Europe and many old and famous States have fallen or may fall into the grip of the Gestapo and all the odious apparatus of Nazi rule, we shall not flag or fail. We shall go on to the end, we shall fight in France, we shall fight on the seas and oceans, we shall fight with growing confidence and growing strength in the air, we shall defend our island, whatever the cost may be, we shall fight on the beaches, we shall fight on the landing grounds, we shall fight in the fields and in the streets, we shall fight in the hills;* ***we shall never surrender.***

On October 29, 1941, 40 days before the U.S. entered World War II, Churchill visited the Harrow School to hear the traditional songs he had sung there as a youth, as well as to speak to the student body. Part of the speech he gave has become an oft-repeated call to never quit—in other words, to have Grit:

Never give in. Never give in; never, never, never, never—in nothing, great or small, large or petty—never give in, except to convictions of honor and good sense. Never yield to force. Never yield to the apparently overwhelming might of the enemy.

As I think about Churchill and World War II, I am reminded of a note I received recently from a conference attendee, Karen Hawes, the county manager for Lee County Administration. She wrote, "Those three words—Vision, Mindset and Grit—are what have been missing in our society for many years. Two weeks ago, I lost my mum-in-law, Sybil, who was from England. She was a great lady, serving in the WRAF in WW II. As I listened to Scott, it occurred to me that our parents and grandparents had the Vision, Mindset and Grit after WW II to get out of the Depression, so we can do the same."

Never Give Up

The notion of never giving up, never surrendering in the face of overwhelming adversity, must seem like sheer madness to many people. Yet, nearly every breakthrough usually involves ordinary people performing the extraordinary. Think of Roger Bannister, the athlete who finally broke the record for the four-minute mile. Do we think people like Bannister have been specially endowed and simply use their extraordinary powers to overcome huge obstacles? Let's not make the mistake of discounting the spectacular feats of ordinary people on the assumption they were secretly extraordinary to begin with. I believe ordinary people who accomplish the extraordinary recognize that, despite all circumstances, they must persevere until they succeed. They must use Grit day after day, month after month, year after year.

These people—like Mark Zuckerberg, best known for co-founding and leading Facebook—adopt a never-give-up attitude, which can best be described by one word: Grit. They develop the Mindset that they will follow a specific direction to accomplish their dream. They have a passion and a Vision, and they Grip onto it and make a choice not to give up until they succeed.

Mental Resolve

Grit requires mental resolve, but how often do we mistake experiencing recurring thoughts for real thinking and reflection? We could make profound differences in how our lives unfold, as opposed to being subject to the whims and vagaries of each passing day, by reflecting and taking time each day to pause and just think. At 19, I made decisions and thought in ways that would fortify me for the long, challenging decades to come. I learned to have mental resolve, to have Grit, to determine never to quit, give up or surrender. In many ways, I have been lucky. The mental resolve and Grit I formulated at age 19 have carried me through to age 53 and, no doubt, will sustain me at 67, perhaps even 87 and longer. Why 87? It's my football number.

Imagine what you can accomplish if you are willing to put your Grit into action!

"Strength does not come from physical capacity.
It comes from an indomitable will."
– Gandhi

VISION

Study your hand. See how your fingers operate independently of each other. Now notice how they are all connected at the palm. Think of your team, your organization. Metaphorically, the fingers are the team members and the palm is the organization—the entity that holds them all together.

● ● ● ●

MINDSET

The Mindset of never giving up, never quitting, is the Mindset of a champion.

● ● ● ●

GRIT

Is as much a habit as failing is.

CHAPTER 7

WHY VERSUS WHAT

Forty-five days had passed after my accident and I had survived all my spinal cord related complications. I was finally strong enough to undergo a lengthy six-and-a-half-hour spinal fusion surgery by Dr. Stringer and his team at Bay Medical Community Hospital. They began by making an incision starting from the back of my neck at the cervical 2 vertebra level and down to the thoracic 1 level. After they peeled back the layers, they could see that my C6 vertebra was fractured on the left side and both the C6 and the C7 vertebrae were loose. They opened up the left posterior of my back to my chest to expose a rib, cut it out and began the fusion of my neck.

A few days after surgery, my nurse noticed blood in my stool. I was bleeding internally. My doctors performed an arthroscopy, a minimally invasive surgical procedure, to scout around and found I had developed three bleeding stomach ulcers. One of them was large and becoming a big concern. They decided to medicate me first, knowing that if the medication did not work they would have no choice but to cut a hole through my belly, into my stomach to stop the ulcers from growing and bleeding. Fortunately, over the coming week the medication worked and I was able to avoid additional surgery.

Facing the Mask

On the 21st of December, the anesthesiologist came into my room and said, "Scott, we have a serious problem." He reported that the oxygen level in my red blood cells was way below normal. Red blood cells transport oxygen throughout the body and remove carbon dioxide. Not removing enough carbon dioxide from your body can be fatal. He said, "We need to get a large quantity of pure oxygen into your system over the next 24 hours to right the problem. There are only two methods to tackle this problem. The first choice is we can hook you up to a machine to breathe for you, using a tracheotomy tube. This would require minor surgery by cutting a hole in your throat to insert a tube into your lungs. The second option is to put a mask over your face for you to breathe on your own. However, there is a catch."

Do you ever notice there is *always* a catch when it comes to someone else's ideas?

He said, "Since your lungs are so weak from your paralysis, you would need to stay awake for the next 24 hours straight and monitor every single breath to ensure you are inhaling as much pure oxygen as possible." He turned away and, as he was leaving my room, said, "I'll give you 10 minutes to decide what *you* want to do."

Quick Decisions

Sometimes in life we have to make decisions quickly, but why can't we make more decisions quickly? Why do we have to think and worry so much? This goes back to Mindset. It was during those 10 minutes so many years ago that I believed the doctor, my anesthesiologist, was giving me an opportunity to make a decision to stand up to the challenge at hand. Then I realized that if I was not willing to stand up to the challenge, take an informed risk and call up every last ounce of Grit, I would be risking even more. So, I made the decision to use the oxygen mask. I will have you know it was one of the longest, most painstaking 24-hour periods of my life as I fought for every single breath while trying to stay awake.

I was in intensive care, and several hours into this process there seemed to be no end. Even when I passed the halfway mark I felt little solace. My nurse came in intermittently to see how I was doing, take blood and update her chart. My Vision was clear. I knew what I wanted to happen as an end result. I continuously kept my Mindset on the task and was determined, no matter how difficult the 24-hour journey, to Grit it out.

No Blame Game

During my time under the mask, fighting for every deep breath, I thought a lot about what had happened. Within two weeks of the accident, after I had come out of my medicated state, I learned that Ed, my friend who was driving, was wearing his seat belt and had survived with minor bumps and bruises as well as a torn ACL. I also remembered that the two of us had been drinking.

What's ironic about that is this: Four years leading up to college, I worked for my dad, who was the golf course superintendent at Turtle Creek Country Club. Like many organizations, Turtle Creek cared about their people, their safety and the safety of others. Some of my job responsibilities involved driving trucks and operating heavy equipment as well as being around and applying hazardous fertilizers and chemicals. Because of this, Turtle Creek made a point to educate and reeducate me on the importance of following safety procedures, protocols and measures. Organizations such as theirs routinely encourage you to be safe and watch out for others and stress the importance of wearing your personal protective equipment (PPE). Depending on the industry, PPE might mean steel-toe boots, fire-resistant clothing, safety glasses, safety face mask, hard hat, gloves and wearing your seat belt whether you are the driver or passenger.

Realizing I had this safety knowledge, or should I say, this safety Mindset, hit me square in the chest. My split-second decision not to wear my seat belt riding passenger in Ed's car left me paralyzed from the chest down.

And when I crossed that 24-hour breathing finish line with every last ounce of Grit I could muster, I came to believe that you cannot always predict the outcomes of the choices you make in your life or in your work; however, you can always take responsibility for those outcomes as opposed to blaming others when things don't go as you planned. That was when I made the decision to take ownership over what had happened to me as opposed to putting all the blame on Ed.

Defining Moments

This became a defining moment in my life—a moment that gave me the courage to let it happen, let go of the past, focus on the now and begin the fight of a lifetime to prove what I am being told cannot be done.

I find that sharing this with others when I'm delivering a speech has a major impact on their lives. A note I received from DeAnne, a conference attendee at a major university, confirms this. She wrote, "Scott, you taught us how to reach deep within ourselves and resource the reserve needed to survive and prevail instead of being a victim!"

What Questions

It was during that same time I made the decision to change my Mindset and stopped asking the *Why* questions as they related to my current challenges, such as, "Why did this happen to me?" or "Why does life have to be this hard, this painful and difficult?" Instead, I started asking the *What* questions inspired by my days of studying the martial arts, such as, "What can I do to aid my recovery?" and "What can I gain if I'm willing to embrace my paralyzing experience instead of resisting it?" Then I made the commitment to act on those questions. Going down that road of trials and tribulations, successes and failures, I learned the *What* questions have a tendency to create forward momentum. You might be surprised to learn how easy it is to stay in those questioning stages, particularly when things are not going exactly as you had planned.

Answering with Action

The next time you ask *Why* to any of your ongoing challenges, notice how it becomes a vicious cycle, leaving you more frustrated than ever before. The next time you are experiencing pain in your life from a failed relationship, financial difficulties or even the pain of losing unexpected business to your competition, notice that asking *Why* doesn't solve anything. The *Why* questions you form when challenged lead to a dead end, not solutions, and they can't help you overcome your pain.

In that 21st hour fighting for every breath and tired beyond belief, the decision to take accountability and change my Mindset to start asking *What* rather than *Why* questions had a significant influence on my life that day, the next and even today, decades later. I know from the bottom of my heart it will have the same impact on your life. Take a moment and think about the *Why* questions you may be asking yourself. Do they sound something like "Why does life have to be this hard?" or "Why did I get passed up on a promotion?" or "Why isn't my business doing better?" How about if you are in sales: "Why don't I have better numbers this month?" or "Why aren't I hitting my targeted projections?"

Whatever your *Why* questions are, turn them into *What* questions. For example, "What can I do to make things better in my life, both personally and professionally?" "What actions can I take to change my results?" Write the *What* questions down. Fight for them by deciding here and now that every time a *Why* question pops into your mind, you will immediately transform it into a *What* question you wrote. As you learn to do this, you will begin to see forward momentum. Be persistent as you go through this process and be willing to let things go by taking a different approach when you meet resistance. Recognize when you are spinning your wheels, then change your course and explore uncharted waters.

Mount Everest and Back

If you want a fresh Vision, if you truly want to transform your Mindset, you must be willing to be Gritty at times and persevere. Ask the *What* questions rather than the *Why* questions when you are frustrated, discouraged or when your challenges seem to outweigh your opportunities. If you change your way of thinking, this strategy can become one of your most defining moments too.

Prior to donning my oxygen mask, my high school and college sweetheart walked into intensive care and gave me a present—a little stuffed bear. She then pressed the back of the bear to open its arms, and when she released the button the bear had gripped onto one of many lifesaving plastic tubes filled with medicine two feet above me. For 24 painstaking hours, we, the bear and I, worked together monitoring every single breath. Staying awake for 24 hours is hard enough, but especially difficult when you are lying flat on your back. With the mask over my face, that day became the longest 24-hour stretch of my life, but one of the most fruitful and rewarding.

When it was over, I felt as if I had crawled to the top of Mount Everest and back again—without climbing equipment. With this grueling task completed, my doctors ran tests and gave me the good news. The oxygen in my blood had reached the appropriate level and my situation had stabilized—no hole in my throat, no more face mask. Another milestone reached and passed. Even so, I knew I was still in for the fight of my life.

Breakfast of Champions

I took a meaningful and calculated risk and had the Grit to follow through during those 24 hours, and the experience was beyond rewarding. For the next three days my body demanded rest, and I complied. As I continued to heal, I wondered if the next meal would stay down, and my thoughts drifted once again.

A New Hero for an 8-Year-Old

When I was 8 years old, I had been introduced to martial arts, a style known as Kyuki-Do tae kwon do, by Royal West, our family's next-door neighbor in Lake Geneva, Wisconsin. I will never forget that day as long as I live. He took our class to see a new movie, *Enter the Dragon,* an over-the-top karate action film featuring Bruce Lee, a legend in the art. Bruce Lee became my new hero and Tae kwon do became a defining sport for me.

Tae kwon do teaches you to know your strengths and your weaknesses, as well as those of your competitors. You learn to believe in yourself and push beyond the expected by opening your mind and expanding your horizons. Back in Wisconsin, Royal told us, "If you want to progress, you must set high goals, maintain a positive attitude and persevere 100% of the time. Discipline will help get you there, and it will be constantly reinforced as you learn to become assertive without being domineering."

Imagine the Outcomes

Martial arts taught me the benefits of leaving my comfort zone at an early age, and the cold weather in Wisconsin forced my dad out of his. When I was still 8, my dad got tired of the cold and moved our family to Stuart, Florida, a small town on the Atlantic seaboard.

My parents enrolled me in a new style of martial arts, Pai Lum Kung Fu, with Jim Wilson as my new instructor, who we called Si-Fu, the name given to a Kung Fu teacher. His brother, Don "The Dragon" Wilson, is an amazing martial artist as well. During Don's occasional visits to our class, we would spar, which is controlled fighting with no contact to the head. Don's drive and tenacity was inspiring to me. He dedicated himself to his sport and competed tirelessly to become a Champion International Kickboxer. He has appeared in 35 movies, including *Say Anything* with John Cusack, *Batman Forever* with Val Kilmer and Nicole Kidman, and *White Tiger*.

As I mentioned earlier, one of the things I learned in the martial arts was never to lose the ability to be a student; always seeking, always asking: *What do I not know? What am I missing? What can I practice next?* I also learned to stop worrying about yesterday and focus totally on the task at hand today. This brings us back to the *What* questions.

Rather than meandering about, asking yourself *Why* questions relating to your challenges, use *What* questions to derive specific action steps to decide what you would do next time. This has been a powerful tool in helping me succeed in life.

VISION

Answer three *What* questions about your Vision.
What do I really enjoy doing? What do I care
deeply about? What tasks am I doing that
I would like to hand off to someone else?

● ● ● ●

MINDSET

Take three *What* questions and write
them as specific action steps you can
take to create forward momentum.

● ● ● ●

GRIT

Have the Grit to move on your action steps.
Keep going even when it is difficult or tedious.
A life of forward momentum awaits you,
but it takes persistence to break away from
the *Why* and look at the *What* in life.

CHAPTER 8

THINK OUTSIDE THE MOMENT

ecovering on many fronts, I was preparing myself mentally to be transferred to Craig Hospital in Englewood, Colorado, known as the best spinal cord rehabilitation center in the country. Fortunately, I was still covered under my dad's health insurance and they agreed to fund the expense.

One morning, prior to being transferred to Colorado, Dr. Stringer came in during his rounds and grabbed my right big toe, as he did every morning. Typically, he would then ask me to move it. I would always close my eyes and push as hard as I could, but nothing would happen. On that particular day, I asked for pillows to be placed behind my back to prop me up so I could see my toes. I thought if I could see them, maybe I would have a better chance of moving them.

With total concentration and every last ounce of energy I could muster, I pushed as hard as I could. To my total amazement, my right big toe moved, just barely—less than one-eighth of an inch, but it moved. Adrenaline rushed through my veins. The news spread as widely and quickly as wildfire. My mom was there with Grandma Alpha, and together they shared the victory and were overwhelmed with joy. Mom telephoned everyone we knew to tell them the great news, including my great uncle Jim. He lives in Quincy, Illinois, with many other of my relatives and has been a great influence in my life. He made the long drive down to be with me for a few weeks with his wife, Aunt Nan. Two amazing people. Uncle Jim inspired me and so many others with one word: *Tremendous!* I don't care what time of day it is or how he is feeling. When you ask, it's always *Tremendous!*

Inner Strength

Dr. Stringer said it had been merely an involuntary reflex, but *I could feel the energy* in my body running down to my toe. I could feel it even though I was numb. My nerves were firing, or I believed they wanted to fire. Mustering up every last ounce of Grit I had, I focused and moved my toe again. I felt as though I had completed a marathon using every ounce of strength and collapsed into a deep sleep for the next three hours. What a day!

So much for the theory on involuntary reflex! At that point my physical and occupational therapists set a variety of small goals for me. I spent every waking moment thereafter pushing myself, seeking to make my toe muscles stronger, using all my physical and mental strength. I Gritted it out until I was fatigued, which seemed to happen quickly.

Physical therapy soon became Pain and Torture in full gear! Every morning when I awoke, I hoped to discover more capability, but over the coming days nothing changed much. I tried desperately not to let the lack of further results affect the optimistic long-term outlook I had gained.

Just a few months prior to my accident, I could take my right leg and perform a roundhouse martial arts kick at full speed, laying the top of my foot within an inch of my opponent's head without ever touching him. Now I was thrilled and very grateful just to be able to move my toe. Yes, my life had changed dramatically. Following my accident, the local newspaper, *The*

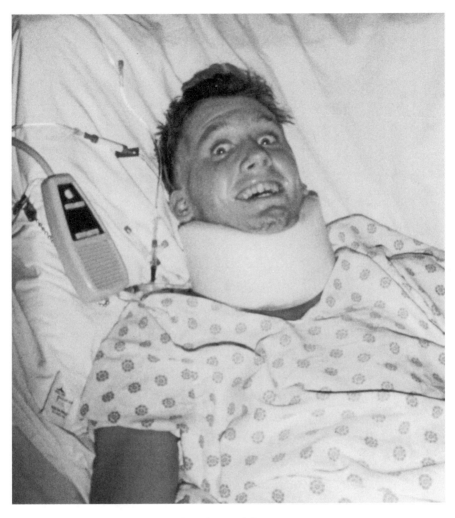

Moved my right toe.

Stuart News, wrote a story about me in its December 27th issue. The writer, Ed Filo, did a nice job and everybody was excited about the piece. He wrote:

> *Friends and relatives of Scott Burrows believe the Martin County teenager's spirit and inner strength will help pull him through the most traumatic period of his*

life…Right now he's concentrating on how to take care of himself. "He was able to sit up in a chair the other day and move his head and arms. It is an accomplishment. But he's not the type to stop there," said Tom Burrows, his father, director of the Turtle Creek Club in Tequesta. It is quite a change for a youngster who enjoyed physical sports like football and karate…Scott graduated from Martin County High School in 1983, where he lettered as a tight end for the Tiger football team. He also earned a black belt in Kung Fu and worked his way up to be the state's number one light heavyweight in full-contact karate. At the time of his accident, Scott was majoring in business at Florida State University, where he was a walk-on wide receiver for the Seminoles. The 6-foot-1, 185-pound sophomore was elected in his freshman year as Mr. September for the school calendar. Wanda Yarborough, Martin County High School principal, described him as "an unofficial and unelected spiritual leader who would direct student cheers while he was on the sidelines…" Chuck McCaughey, who coached Scott in football and full-contact karate, described him as a strong-willed, likable and dedicated youngster who enjoyed physical contact just for the challenge. "Pound for pound, he was dynamite. But he was not one of those guys who went looking for a fight. He liked to talk—he'd talk a mile a minute. If you met him, you would just like Scott." Tom Burrows said he does not know how long it will be before Scott returns home, but has unfailing confidence his strong-willed son will return to school and finish college. "He intends to. That is what he said. And knowing him, he will do it one way or another."

The Athlete Within

Lying on my back reading that article, all I could think about was how physically active I had been before my injury. As an incoming high school freshman, I had never played organized football, but had always wanted to. With my parents' blessing, I attended tryouts and made the team. I poured my heart into football, learning all I could about becoming an effective team player and excelling at the positions to which I was assigned by my coaches.

Having a tenacious Vision, the right Mindset and Tremendous Grit helped me ultimately to become a four-year starter. As I entered my junior year in high school, my wide receiver football coach, Chuck McCaughey, who was also a martial arts instructor, presented an irresistible offer to me. He asked if I would be interested in kickboxing and competing in the Professional Kickboxing Association. He offered to train me. This was another dream coming true for me. I accepted his offer in a heartbeat and began training.

It soon became apparent that I had become overconditioned for "tournament" fighting, meaning no contact with the opponent's head and, no matter how hard I tried, I could not follow through with a punch or kick to someone's head. Good habit or bad? It all depends who you ask.

Coach McCaughey realized that my reluctance to strike the head area would be a lingering issue if we did not clear it up. He brought in a friend of mine, Mickey, an accomplished boxer. With our gloves and pads in place, the first time we fought, he

Chuck McCaughey and me.

attacked me. Mickey hit me so hard I saw stars. Then, between rounds, loud enough so I could hear, my coach yelled, "Knock Scott out."

Mickey came at me like a raging bull. His attack was ferocious. He hit me in the head again and again. I became furious and fought back with everything I had. I hit him with a shot to the head, and he went reeling. I had knocked *him* out. In that moment, I realized I had broken through my self-imposed barrier of not being able to follow through. I had reconditioned myself, and it became a major turning point.

Fight or Flight

Later that year I was pitted against a 32-year-old karate instructor who had decided to take up kickboxing. Although this was his first kickboxing fight, he had fighting experience as a Golden Gloves boxing champion; even so, at the end of three three-minute rounds, I won the match by a unanimous decision.

By the time I was a freshman in college I had won my first two kickboxing fights. As a Florida State University freshman football player, my priorities changed slightly and kickboxing took a back seat, but my thirst for it returned directly after we finished football spring training. Some people say competition is in my blood!

My freshman year at Florida State, Coach McCaughey called. He said, "I can arrange a fight in your old high school gym. Would you be interested?" Because of college football, I had not trained or fought in a kickboxing match in nearly eight months, but the idea of a new fight was too enticing. I trained

Me against the 32-year-old kickboxer.

on campus, hoping to be in the best kickboxing shape possible. I will never forget the day I was training for my upcoming match in Kellum Hall at FSU. A guy I met on campus, a boxer, offered to train and spar with me. We were in the only open space we could find, right in front of the elevators. We both fought hard, but ironically I knocked him out by accident. It did feel good, however, to know I had that potential. A few weeks later, it was go time. Chuck, my karate trainer, and John Salvador, one of

my best friends, gave me a pep talk before I entered the ring. My opponent and I began the match by touching gloves and bowing. Forty-two seconds later I knocked him out. I had achieved the win I was fighting for

Kickboxing – ESPN

and had also stretched my Vision. Another match was scheduled in less than a month at the West Palm Beach Auditorium; ESPN would film the event. That match was broadcast on national television, and I won in a unanimous decision.

Big-Time College Football

In my senior year in high school I already knew I wanted to be a star athlete in football. I knew I needed to give myself that extra edge to be extraordinary, so I tried out for the high school track team to stay in shape and increase my speed on the field. By the end of the season I had competed in six different events and broken records in both the 440-yard relay and the triple jump. I went on to compete in the 880-yard relay in the State Finals, and we finished in 5th place. During our annual awards banquet, I was selected MVP by my peers.

I turned down several football scholarships offered to me by the smaller division colleges. I had larger than life aspirations. With my parents' blessings, I enrolled at Florida State University and tried out for the team as a walk-on wide receiver. The school was on the verge of becoming a big football powerhouse. As history shows, it went on to stay at the top for more than two decades under legendary head coach Bobby Bowden.

Gridiron Fever

Few walk-ons ever get field-play time, but I never let that become a distraction. I will never forget going to the office of Coach Billy Sexton, the walk-on coach, and challenging him to give me a shot at making the team. After a *lively* conversation, he led me to the equipment room, where I was given a full set of gear. When I entered the locker room, I felt like I had stepped into Wonderland. It was huge. The locker of Greg Allen, a Heisman trophy candidate, was one row down from mine. So were the lockers of star players such as Martin Mayhew, Willis "Weegie" Thompson, Hassan Jones, Jessie Hester, Garth Jax, all of whom would go on to play in the NFL in years to come. Steve Nicklaus, a notable wide receiver and son of golfing great Jack Nicklaus, was

Senior Year of High School: One of my best friends, John Salvador (right), and me.

two rows over. I was not recruited like these guys had been, nor was I offered a scholarship. No one had ever heard my name or seen me play. Nevertheless, I entered the program with tons of confidence. I just simply believed I had the skills to compete and make the team. My goal was to prove any naysayers wrong. What an opportunity!

"Courage is being scared to death, but saddling up anyway."
—*John Wayne*

No Cakewalk

Walk-ons are treated like raw meat. They are put on a third- or fourth-string team across the scrimmage line from a first- or second-string team. They attempt to block opponents as much as 75 pounds heavier who are trying to flatten them like a steamroller. Having run track the previous spring in high school helped considerably. I had clocked in at 4.6 seconds in the 40-yard dash. My time was equal to what some NFL players currently run, although they have to be down to about 4.2 or 4.1 if they are going to carry the ball. Each tenth of a second at that distance translates to almost a yard. That means the difference between being tackled and leaving the opponent in the dust.

As team members, we had to learn to pull ourselves up and make it through practice under all conditions. If we sustained a cut, we still played. If we got hurt and could still play, we did. We played not only for ourselves, but for everyone around us. Third string or not, we knew the rest of the team was counting on us. The first stringers needed the rest of us to challenge them to the best of their ability so they would be better prepared for game situations.

Although I trained as hard as any player on the team, I did not suit up for home games or travel with the team on away games. I knew in the back of my mind that would come in time. Still, I was honored to be part of a 9-4 season that culminated in our victorious appearance in the Peach Bowl in Atlanta. I was the recipient of a Peach Bowl watch, a gold band with a white face and gold letters that read "Peach Bowl" with a football and stars on the top.

The Price of Victory

In the spring of that year, we prepared for football training camp. We entered what head coach Bobby Bowden called the "Tuff Twenty," an intense 20-day training session. Many players have a difficult time completing this training due to injury, heat or physical exhaustion. My Vision was to make an impression on the coaches. My Mindset was to stay focused. My Grit was to never give up. At the end of the 20 days, I was honored to earn a Tuff Twenty T-shirt given to those who make every single practice. Very few players ever receive this award.

The following day, Coach Bowden held his annual Garnet & Gold Scrimmage with the Florida State offense against the Florida State defense. Because non-scholarship players like me would get a look from each of the coaches, we took this particular scrimmage very seriously. We were competing with guys who already had starting positions, and we wanted to look good.

Sporting my Tuff 20 T-shirt for inspiration

Know Thy Competitor

Whether you are an athlete, a student, in sales, a manager, president or CEO of a company, or if you work on the front lines, you can never rest on your laurels. Your competition is always coming after you. They are getting stronger and more fierce, and they are learning from you. That's why you have to know your Vision and what you are always fighting for. You need the right Mindset to show up every day and stay focused on task while raising the bar, and at times you have to get Gritty. If you don't, you may be left behind.

You have to know your competitors to play your best against them. To prepare for a college football game, each team watches game footage of its opposition. They review plays and individual performances to improve their chance of winning on game day. Learning about your competition always gives you a competitive edge, even in the real world.

If you're in business, do you take the time to study your competition so you are well versed in their strengths and weaknesses as well as those of their organization? Do you know their products and services as well as your own, and can you fully articulate their benefits as well as their detriments? You must do this because the best of your competitors are learning the same about you.

Samurai

Chuck Laughlin, author of *Samurai Selling,* asked, "Did you ever lose a sale to an inferior product, an inferior competitor or an inferior company?" Of course, if you are in sales you know that has happened to all of us. Selling is a battle of the mind. Above all, you have to have the right attitude each and every time you make contact with a prospect. Attitudes are contagious. Recall the last five people you have met. Are you better off for having met them? More importantly, are they better or worse off for having met you?

Laughlin suggested that just as water has the ability to take the shape of its container, you have to be flexible in your approach to people. Not everyone responds similarly. However, most people are pleased when you do the unexpected, solidify the connection, make the point and convey the benefits of what you have to offer. Even when you are pitted against seemingly superior products or services, you must believe in your company and yourself and allow your prospect to feel your commitment. Your spirit is stronger than anything your competitor can pull out of his bag.

Priorities Aligned

After the journey of all the events leading up to the magical 1983 season at Florida State, my GPA unfortunately suffered and was now a 2.0. Over the summer, my parents had a long talk with me and said that I had to make a decision to focus on my grades and just one sport. In the back of my mind, I knew I had to do that and also knew it would be a tough decision. I thought about my life, what I was fighting for and believed I could take kickboxing to the next level. Before I made that decision on summer break, I was receiving mail every other week from the FSU coaches. Mickey Andrews, an assistant football coach, wrote a letter to the team during the spring that was as forceful as it was inspiring. He wrote,

> *"This is the time of the year when everyone has 'good intentions'...The difference between winners and losers is those who take action to work toward their goals as opposed to those who merely dream about them... So it comes down to this...Are you preparing to be a champion? Your teammates are!"*

I saved all the letters from the coaches. Those were some of the best college football coaches in the country. They had honed and refined their messages over the years so it would sink in and make an indelible impression upon the young men they coached. Years later, it struck me that any team, sports or other, could draw inspiration from elements in these letters.

Billy Sexton, my walk-on coach, wrote, "People are thermometers or thermostats. Are you a thermometer, one who simply records the highs or lows, or are you a thermostat who reacts to situations by trying to improve things?" My days of playing college football taught me that being a thermostat gives you the competitive edge. How could being a thermostat impact your life today?

The Man in the Glass

John Eason, my wide receiver coach, sent a letter telling us, "We are excited about the potential your team has along with the challenges and demands that go along with having a great year."

He then offered a list typifying the habits of a loser, at least as far as a team is concerned. For example, "The loser goes with the tide. He is a know-it-all, he does not listen and he does not accept new ideas. He is a rebel; he works by himself. He never tries to take the lead; he merely follows the crowd, generally behind them. He is Joe Milquetoast, a watcher, worried about what other people think. He cuts corners when he can, ducks out of practice, is always ready with an excuse and always plays the hypochondriac. The loser is a complainer as well; he gives up easily and allows himself to be distracted from the job at hand. He might look good against weak competition, but he will look bad against strong competition. On top of it all, he is a quitter. He does not stick it out till the end. He will start the job, but he will not finish. You cannot count on him; he is unreliable."

Coach Eason ended with a famous poem, called "The Guy in the Glass" written by Dale Wimbrow in 1934. The poem was taken from the book titled *The Edge*, compiled by Howard K. Ferguson, and the full poem is easily found on the internet.

It begins:

When you get what you want in your struggle for pelf*
And the world makes you King for a day,
Then go to the mirror and look at yourself,
And see what that guy has to say.
The poem ends with the stanza:
You can fool the world down the pathway of years,
And get pats on the back as you pass,
But your final reward will be heartaches and tears,
If you've cheated the guy in the glass.

*money and riches, often ill-gotten

As I lay on my bed staring at the ceiling, I marveled at how mere months ago those letters and messages had been so motivating to me. Surprisingly, even in my paralyzed state, those letters and messages still had a strong impact on me. I was reminded of one of the oldest success quotes in the sporting and business world I had heard so many times: "Winners never quit and quitters never win!"

During my time at FSU, being around the most motivating coaches in the world, as well as my teammates, was a rewarding and enriching experience that would serve me well in the coming months and for the rest of my life.

VISION
Dream.

• • • •

MINDSET
Plan.

• • • •

GRIT
Get there.

CHAPTER 9

IN FOR THE LONG HAUL

The Money Pit

My parents came with me as I flew via air ambulance from Bay Medical Community Hospital to Craig Hospital in Denver, Colorado. Unfortunately, the insurance company denied the claim my parents so desperately needed. The one-way plane ticket to Denver alone cost $5,000, a small fortune in 1984 dollars, and my parents were not wealthy. To put this into perspective, in 2018 dollars, the cost of that one-way flight, adjusted to healthcare inflation, would be $38,000 at minimum. That cost was yet another of many unexpected expenses my parents were facing based on my split-second decision to not wear my seat belt. Friends of the family were

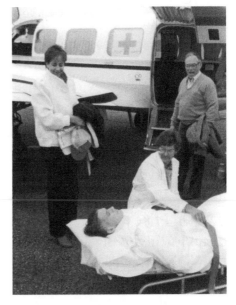

Mom and I getting ready to board the air ambulance to take us to Craig Hospital in Denver, Colorado, where my rehabilitation would begin.

busy promoting fund-raising events every month to help meet unexpected financial obligations related to my accident for which my parents were liable. To meet many of those expenses, my parents had no choice but to deplete my college fund and their retirement savings, as well as to sell as many assets as they could. My family had to raise cash.

The air ambulance medical team consisted of staff trained in flight physiology, including a registered nurse, a respiratory therapist and a registered flight paramedic. Why all the fuss for a flight? At high altitudes, things can quickly go wrong for someone in my condition.

Joy Ride

At this point my parents had developed nerves of steel—or so we thought. In less than two months, their finances had been upended and my father had scrambled all over creation to maintain his professional responsibilities. They now were in for the unanticipated roller-coaster ride of their lives. The weather was foul, the flight was rough, and we landed three times before reaching Denver, Colorado. I was medicated to the hilt and yet was still extremely uncomfortable. My parents said it was the worst ride of their lives.

Around 7:00 p.m., after a daylong ordeal, our perilous journey to Oz was finally over; we had arrived at Craig Hospital. The next day, Dr. Luke told us my spinal cord injury was a catastrophic disability involving all bodily systems. He explained that I must be ready to make dramatic lifestyle changes and prepare myself mentally because the road to recovery at Craig Hospital might be more than six months.

As Dr. Luke further explained, Craig Hospital was designed to help patients prepare for what they will do when they return home, such as handling money, working with a live-in caregiver, taking care of their own needs and responding to friends as a quadriplegic. Family support, he explained, would be essential. All the same, upon entering Craig Hospital, I told my dad, "When I leave here, I will walk out that front door." Despite my desperate situation, I was determined to walk again. Perhaps that was a cocky statement given my paralyzed state, but it's how I felt and what I believed on the inside.

Grounded Again

My rehabilitation started with yet another unexpected challenge, another serious, life-threatening complication. I was placed on a tilt bed, designed to gently rise vertically. The purpose of the bed was to help me become accustomed again to gravity, but I started feeling nauseous and dizzy and was having trouble breathing. My doctor took out his stethoscope and said, "Take a deep breath and blow it out, again and again." He then asked me, "Do you smoke?" I answered, "No," and in that moment the look on his face became serious and I was rushed to have a chest X-ray. The results revealed that a blood clot had lodged in my left lung. The medical term is *pulmonary embolism,* the same type of embolism that took the life of 39-year-old NBC-TV correspondent David Bloom while he was covering the war in Iraq in 2003.

Derrick Thomas, who played professional football for the Kansas City Chiefs, had a similar experience with a pulmonary embolism. On February 8, 2000, he was in an automobile accident, broke his neck and was diagnosed a quadriplegic. While being transferred to therapy in his wheelchair, he told his mother he didn't feel well just before his eyes rolled back. He went into cardiac arrest and died as a result of a pulmonary embolism.

To say the least, my situation was grave. I was confined to bed rest for another 11 consecutive days. I was not to be moved at all to prevent the blood clot from becoming dislodged, traveling to my heart and causing a fatal cardiac arrest. My doctor administered Coumadin, a blood thinner designed to dissolve the clot. I was lucky and the drug ultimately worked. Again, I had hope and prayed that I would survive.

Every Day is a New Day

On the 12th day, still alive, thankful and feeling blessed, it was time to become reacquainted with the tilt bed. I only vomited once. Each day thereafter brought new challenges. At this point, the only action I could complete independently was to call for help. There was a ball attached to a string hanging from the ceiling within my reach. When I moved my arm to touch it, a light went on signaling the nursing station to come to my room. Customer service at its best!

The daily physical rehabilitation program became my routine, my challenge and, ultimately, my salvation. My typical day started at 7:00 a.m. I would eat, get dressed with the help of an aide and go to therapy for 60 to 90 minutes. After therapy, I ate lunch, slept, went back to therapy and then slept again. I remember sleeping after each session. I had given my all in therapy, and

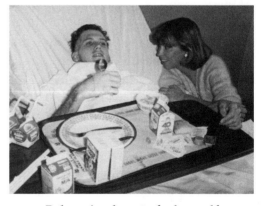

Relearning how to feed myself.

the hours of sleep came easily to me. I began to strengthen the muscles in my arms that were coming back to help carry the weight for those that remained dormant.

VISION

Be courageous enough to include
the impossible in your vision.

● ● ● ●

MINDSET

Welcome unexpected challenges.

● ● ● ●

GRIT

Stay alive.

CHAPTER 10

RECAPTURING THE MINDSET

As Far As You Will Ever Go

On January 20, 1985, I turned 20. On my birthday, Dad came over to me to give me what I expected to be a big hug. Instead, he wrapped his arms under my arms and hoisted me to an upright position, holding my limp body firmly in his arms. It was an amazing feeling that reinforced my Vision of standing again on my own.

Dad is holding me up. I cannot stand, and my feet are not touching the floor.

The day after my birthday, my parents returned home to Florida for a few weeks. After they had left, I was alone when one of my doctors told me something I was totally unprepared to handle. His words sent me into a tailspin like a sucker punch to the midsection. Following my physical therapy session, the doctor pulled me aside and said, "Scott, I've had the opportunity to get to know you, your sporting background and the positive attitude you

98

continue to possess. However, I believe you need to understand the seriousness of your spinal cord injury and come to realize that the movement you are now getting back in your arms is not uncommon—but that's as good as it will ever get." Now, I don't know if that is exactly what the doctor said, but what I heard is that I should give up on the idea of progressing further.

If Dreams Die

The truth is, I'm not sure if that's exactly what he said, but that's what I heard. The problem was that I bought into what he was preaching and abandoned my Vision. I was devastated. Everything I had envisioned disappeared into a sinkhole. I fell into a deep state of depression. To make matters worse, my parents were 2,000 miles away in Florida and I had stopped returning their phone calls. My parents called to check on me several times each day.

By the end of the fourth day after that world-shattering statement, my father had had enough of my not returning their calls. He phoned the head nurse and demanded she put me on the phone. He asked me what was wrong and I broke down crying. Reluctantly, I told him, "This is my battle, not yours." I told him I had put them through enough and didn't want to drag them into any more of my problems. My dad, who is an unbelievable listener, heard me out, not saying a word until I was done.

Do Not Buy In

I reluctantly explained to him what the doctor had said to me. When I was done sobbing, he said, "Look, I just visited you last week on your 20th birthday. Your attitude was through the roof, your spirits were high, and your Vision was crystal clear. I know you are down right now, but do me a favor, go back and recapture that Mindset you had on your birthday and make it yours again. Will you do that for me? In the meantime, don't be upset with me, but I am going to have a word with that doctor."

The next morning when I awoke, I couldn't believe my eyes. My dad was standing in the doorway looking back at me. His presence allowed me to believe again that everything would be okay. My dad proved to me that day that anyone can change their way of thinking whether you are in college, a stay-at-home mom, a teacher, a front-line employee, a manager, a VP of sales, a CEO or a 20-year-old quadriplegic. You can always change your way of thinking. Sometimes in life when things are spinning out of control—in our relationships, our finances, our personal and professional lives—we need that one person we can turn to who tells us everything will be okay.

That was when I made a decision: I was *willing to fail, but I was unwilling to quit*. This is the Mindset I took on, and it is the same kind of Mindset you can use to encourage yourself and other people on *your* team to rethink their own possibilities. It's a Mindset that can keep you focused as you unleash your own unique composite of skills, drive and talent upon your community, your marketplace and the world.

Willing to Fail, Unwilling to Quit

A Mindset that is willing to fail, but unwilling to quit will make you more effective and decisive in all areas of your life. By focusing on how you react to problems and how you prepare yourself mentally to take on the next challenge, you will become stronger. As you become stronger in the Mindset of being willing to fail but unwilling to quit, you be better positioned to tap into your unrealized potential. Your production will increase, you will experience greater success, and your satisfaction with life and with your choices will markedly improve.

Flipper vs. the Shark

It was this type of Mindset that got me into scuba diving and spear fishing 10 years after my accident. Although I still battle paralysis in all four of my extremities, over the years I have regained enough arm, hand and finger strength to propel myself underwater. With the help of my good friend, Terrill Goldman, we figured out a way for me to load and shoot a speargun.

I know what you might be thinking: Great, the next time you are vacationing in Florida and swimming in the ocean you now have to be on the lookout for an underwater quadriplegic with a loaded speargun in hand!

I will never forget the time I was with a friend in his 25-foot boat, many miles off the coast of Clearwater, Florida at a point where you could no longer see land. We had one of the most amazing experiences of our lives, one of those Oscar-winning moments.

Diving in 100 feet of water off of Salt Island in the British Virgin Islands at the wreck of the Rhone.

Once the anchor was secured, we began assembling our scuba equipment, put it on and plunged into the water. We descended to the bottom, 70 feet beneath the surface, onto a rocky reef loaded with Florida seafood or, as you might call it—sushi!

We loaded our spearguns and the first fish I speared was a red snapper, a Florida delicacy. As I took the fish off my spear, I saw something huge out of the corner of my right eye. I turned and nearly had a heart attack. No more than three feet away was a wild dolphin about six feet in length just staring at me. His look seemed to say, "Are you going to feed me that snapper or what?" Reluctantly, but graciously, I gave it to him.

It was surreal. In that moment I could feel the excitement and adrenaline running through my veins. So, I reloaded my speargun, looked around and took aim at another red snapper to feed the dolphin. I pulled the trigger. Out of the corner of my eye, I saw Flipper, with his long nose, following the spear as it raced on. This time, when our eyes met again, he gave me a different look that clearly stated his disappointment: "Scotty, how in the world did you miss that?" I never imagined myself feeling like a complete idiot in front of a dolphin, but it happened!

Suddenly, 30 feet away appeared a five-foot, blacktip reef shark swimming in large circles around us looking to join in the feeding. We remained calm and, fortunately, Flipper stood up to the challenge. The dolphin was probably more concerned about losing a free meal than he was about fighting a midsized shark. I was extremely fearful being at such a great depth that I couldn't even see the surface of the water, but once again Mindset came into play.

I had the Mindset to put myself in a position to learn how to scuba dive, spear a fish and feed a wild dolphin 70 feet beneath the surface. Then the shark showed up, but after a few minutes he lost interest and swam off into the abyss. What I have learned about fear is that it is paralyzing.

Fear creates anxiety, concern, worry and nervousness, all negative feelings that keep us paralyzed. When we focus on fear and the negatives, we believe we *can't*. However, I have learned that if you are willing to stand up to your fears and focus on the positives of any situation, you will experience an unbeatable strength that will inspire new thinking and help you find solutions to problems. Most importantly, facing fear keeps you off the sidelines and gets you back in the game of life. When you are in the game, you can explore uncharted waters and find new and different opportunities to overcome challenges. Remember what Helen Hunt said? "I go with what scares me!" Make that principle yours!

David and Goliath

Our second dive that day, believe it or not, proved to be just as heart-pounding as the first. After spearing 20- and 29-inch groupers, a four-foot, 400-pound Goliath grouper showed up to be fed. We felt compelled to oblige, and it quickly became apparent we were going to be the only ones on this trip not enjoying our catch.

Have you ever experienced such a David and Goliath moment in your life? How did you respond? Did you embrace the experience or resist it? This enriching experience following my life-altering accident never would have occurred if I had not been willing to take a risk to become a certified scuba diver and spear fisherman. I made a decision to commit to doing something I had always wanted to do. I stepped outside my comfort zone and transformed the way I thought and what a big step it was. I believe it is important for each of us to seek out experiences that are totally different from our daily routine. That's how we grow.

That day we had an adventure I will remember throughout my life. I had left my comfort zone and experienced one of the best days of my life. I had had an amazing experience I will treasure that will always remind me that when we try something different and take a risk, we can be rewarded beyond our wildest imagination.

We all know people who draw up wonderful goals, dreams and plans and then sit on them for weeks, months and years. Someone like that might be in your seat right now. How much longer are you willing to dwell in a state of blissful inaction? Are you ready to stand up to the challenge and take your shot?

"I learned that courage was not the absence of fear, but the triumph over it. The brave man is not he who does not feel afraid, but he who conquers that fear." – Nelson Mandela

VISION

When your Vision is gone, recapture the Mindset that you had in place before the Vision was lost. Then you can get your Vision back.

● ● ● ●

MINDSET

If there is someone who believes in you more than you believe in yourself, capture their Mindset and make it your own.

● ● ● ●

GRIT

"Great works are performed not by strength, but perseverance." – SAMUEL JOHNSON

CHAPTER 11

ACHIEVING THE IMPOSSIBLE

The Magic Elixir

positive outlook: Unfortunately, this term often is bandied about and loses its potency. However, when you focus on its meaning, you realize that a positive outlook is one of the single most important elements of life. Without it, how can you propel yourself to push forward? I don't know why so many people dwell on the negative. If you want to focus on the negative, pick up a newspaper—it will not disappoint.

Why does the media focus on negative events—fires, floods, murders and personal tragedies? These negative stories can have a significant impact on our daily lives and our outlook. Where are the positive stories? Surely, they must occur in greater numbers than the disasters. I believe if you expect the worst, you set yourself up to receive the worst! I also believe if you channel the positive, you can soar to new heights.

Both positive and negative statements can be extremely powerful to patients who are trying to heal. In his book *Love, Medicine and Miracles*, Bernie Siegel wrote that even coma patients are affected by such statements. For example, if a doctor in the room said, "This does not look good," the patient will be affected by those words. As a result, Siegel forbade his charges to speak in negative terms within earshot of patients.

Even in 1984, a bevy of books, as well as medical and scientific articles, discussing the mind-body connection were available. Perhaps the doctor who felt compelled to share this negative outlook with me had not encountered any of these, or maybe he was simply attempting to shield me from false hope. To this day, his motives are not clear to me, but the results of his statement were. It was as though he had kicked me when I was down. I had to work hard to recapture my Vision and Mindset.

The Destructive Power of "No"

Keep your eyes open to possibilities even when others tell you not to bother. Too often we are told, usually by well-meaning people, "You are not strong enough." "You will not realize your goals." "You are not smart enough." Sadly, we become numb and paralyzed by the *no's* we hear. By saying *yes*, you set yourself up to beat the odds—not all the time, but enough of the time to make a difference. I believe you can change your life once you are ready to stand up and say, "Yes. I can." As President Franklin D. Roosevelt said, "Above all, try something."

The Tour de France

As arduous as rehab is, the reality of being in a wheelchair for the rest of my life motivated me to keep pushing forward and leaning into my future. I began experiencing the return of some muscle strength in my fingers, biceps, triceps and my lower back, but my stomach muscles remained dormant. Even today, if I am lying on the ground, I am unable to do a sit-up.

With this newfound strength in parts of my body, not uncommon for quadriplegics, I was able to perform activities I never thought I would ever have the opportunity to do again. At that point, my physical and occupational therapists set a variety of mini-goals. Although still very weak, one morning my right leg began to fire back up. Eventually, I was able to lift it six inches off the bed—a monumental feat. Over the coming weeks, with lots of therapy, Leslie started hooking my right leg up to electrodes designed to stimulate and strengthen the muscle. The other goal of electrical stimulation was to try to kick-start the muscles, hoping the brain would recognize the signal again. Slowly, my left leg began to fire back. I was now able to lift it maybe two inches off the bed. At this point, Leslie began helping me transfer from my wheelchair to a stationary bike. She placed me on the seat and strapped my feet into the pedals. My first few attempts to pedal were futile. No matter how hard I tried, I couldn't do it. My right leg did not have the strength to carry the weight of my left leg.

Seeing Results

Over a week into this grueling process, my right leg moved just enough with gravity on my side that it carried my left leg. I had completed a full rotation. My emotions were running high and I was overwhelmed with excitement. For the first few weeks I could only complete two or three rotations. As my endurance and strength increased, my left leg began to show signs of life. When it did, I could pedal up to five minutes before becoming so exhausted that I needed three or four hours of rest to recover from the ordeal. I continued this process day after day. With Grit and determination, I was able to increase my time incrementally by 10 and then 15 minutes.

Never Give Up

This was positive news. I consulted one of my doctors—the *good* one—and asked, "Doc, if I continue to get movement back, what do you think"? The answer was always the same: "It is not uncommon in some cases, such as yourself, to get some movement back, even in all four of your extremities, but what is pretty impossible is for quadriplegics to walk again." Regardless of what was being said, I recalled my dad's words. I never gave up hope, I continued to believe, and I knew I could turn guts into Grit and Grit into results.

Consider your own struggles when, no matter what you try, sometimes nothing seems to work in your favor. You may feel you are not making any headway. Hang in there, because this is par for the course in work and in life. All of a sudden, the results curve begins to shoot upward. Even when you think nothing is working, keep plugging away. Maintain the discipline to persevere. Focusing on those things you can control can put you in position to succeed even further.

Bar Exam

At the end of February 1985, Leslie challenged me to the parallel bars. I could feel the energy and adrenaline running through my veins. She challenged me to see if I could stand on my own with my legs harnessed in support braces. Needless to say, I welcomed the opportunity to *stand up to that challenge*. I will never forget the morning she wheeled me in and two other attendants lifted me out of my wheelchair and into the upright position. The braces on each leg were needed to secure my knees and offer support and balance. What an exhilarating experience! I was on cloud nine. I felt taller, too.

The parallel bars were waist high. I placed my hands around the bar. That was quite the challenge because my fingers were weak and did not work well. Even today, my fingers remain weak. I mentally envisioned my task and put all my strength into my Grip with what little hand strength I had. Standing upright for the first time under my own weight was the most uplifting feeling I have ever experienced.

Strength

Standing in front of me, Leslie said, "Try to take a step with your right leg, then your left leg if you can." With people on both sides ready to catch me if I fell, I forced my right hip forward as hard as I could. My right leg moved forward about

six inches! I could not believe it! It moved! I tried with my left as hard as I could, but nothing happened. I wasn't disappointed, though, and kept telling myself if I worked even harder and continued to follow through with therapy, it would come. I knew it was going to take more time and even more Grit.

Moving my legs and barely standing in the parallel bars was the answer to all my

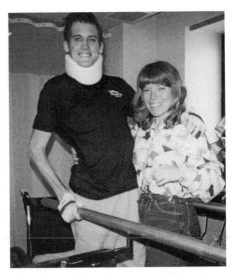

With my physical therapist, Leslie.

prayers. Then it hit me. I was standing almost on my own. I was doing something that people in my condition, from what I was told, rarely, if ever, do. If possible, I became even more intensely focused. I looked forward every day to my time on the parallel bars. It was exhausting, but exhilarating. Each day I excelled a bit more—a six-inch step, an eight-inch step.

However long it took, however hard it seemed, however tedious it was, I exercised seven days a week, including two days every week with or without Karen, my occupational therapist, and Leslie, my physical therapist, helping me strengthen whatever muscles I could. I exerted myself beyond all limits. I called upon every coach and mentor, every training program, every bit of instruction and every last ounce of Grit I had ever experienced to help me move forward.

Karen and Leslie believed in me and challenged me daily. Is there someone like Leslie or Karen challenging and stretching you, believing in you more than you believe in yourself?

Leaving on Foot

When you know your Vision, you have to believe in your heart that your Mindset and Grit can carry you through. March 15, 1984 would be D-Day.

As February turned to March, drawing ever closer to the date of my discharge, my dad returned to Denver a few days early to take me home. He proudly announced what I had said months before: "I will walk out of the front doors of Craig Hospital." That was exactly what I intended to do. It was less than 100 days since I had arrived at Craig Hospital, and it was 52 days since I had been told "You have gone as far as you will ever go."

Slowly, I had been reclaiming highly personal and private activities. I was taking showers with the aid of a shower bench. My wheelchair served as my primary means of mobility. I could stand with braces on my knees and gingerly take small steps with two forearm crutches, otherwise known as Canadian outriggers. I was mentally determined to make my way out of Craig Hospital on my own two feet.

Turning Impossibilities into Possibilities

Dad came into my room early and said, "Are you ready to go home?" You bet I was! I stood up with his help, using my forearm crutches with knee braces secured, and began making my walk down the hallway. He stayed close by my side in case I lost my balance. It was such a great feeling! My walk was not graceful, a bit unorthodox, but I had accomplished what I had been told I would never do: *stand and walk again!*

My father snapped a picture of me walking out of Craig Hospital. It sits on my desk today as a reminder of how far I have come. It is also a gentle reminder of what you can do if you focus on those things you can control as opposed to those things over which you have no control. To this day, I fight paralysis in all four of my extremities. I continue to focus on strengthening my muscles so they can compensate for the weaker muscles and the ones that are still paralyzed.

When we arrived at the Denver Airport, the shuttle driver scurried around to the back for my wheelchair. I said, "No, thank you, I am walking through this airport and to the plane if it kills me." Slowly and most carefully, I made my way, one step at a time, Dad by my side. It seemed like it took forever until we reached the top of the plane's stairs leading into the door. My dad had bought first-class tickets to be certain I would be comfortable. I sat down with the help of my dad and the flight attendant, took a huge breath and quickly fell asleep for the next two hours. I was physically and mentally exhausted. We were going home to Florida!

When You Gotta Go

The flight felt like a victory ride, but soon vivid reminders of the personal challenges ahead could not be ignored. I used an external leg bag. When I woke up, we still had about an hour before reaching Orlando airport. I said to my father, "Hey, Dad, my leg bag is full." His response: "What do you want me to do?" Now I was in a scramble mode.

I told him, "You are going to have to hold me up and walk with me to the bathroom where you will have to lean down by my ankle and release the clip attached to my leg bag so it can be emptied." He said, "We're only an hour from landing; we will take care of it then." As the urge became increasingly uncomfortable, I remember thinking, "Oh man, I have got to release the pressure of this bag before it bursts."

You think you've been in a tight spot?

As inconspicuously as I could, I reached down to my ankle and released the valve. My urine flowed freely onto the carpet along the floor of first class by my window seat. I sat back in my chair with a sigh. My dad looked at me and said, "What are you smiling about?" I sighed again. He said, "What did you do?" I told him I relieved myself. He replied, "You did not, did you?"

To this day, he will say, "Son of a gun, we sat there and no one knew what happened." It was one of those father and son experiences. My dad realized more clearly than before he was dealing with a new son, one he had little experience in helping with day-to-day affairs.

Later, somebody told me a story about an Alan Shepard moment. As the first American in the Mercury Seven program, his initial lift-off time was delayed for 80 minutes due to malfunctioning of a small electrical apparatus. Shepard reported to Gordon Cooper, the prelaunch communicator and a fellow Mercury Seven astronaut, "Man, I gotta pee." "You what?" Cooper exclaimed. "You heard me. I have got to pee. I have been up here forever." There was no procedure, however, for allowing that to happen. The NASA engineers and flight specialists had never planned for that contingency.

Shepard's time in space was only supposed to be minutes. He was to go straight up and return immediately. With time passing and the situation growing urgent, the engineers calculated that if they switched off the power he could relieve himself within his spacesuit and not upset any instrumentation. So, that is exactly what Alan Shepard did. He then lifted off into space, returned to Earth, was picked up by a helicopter and brought to the deck of an aircraft carrier. He waved to the world on camera, smiling the whole time. Trust me, it is a good feeling!

VISION

"If you limit your choices only to what seems possible or reasonable, you disconnect yourself from what you truly want, and all that is left is a compromise." – ROBERT FRITZ

• • • •

MINDSET

"You may have to fight a battle more than once to win it." – MARGARET THATCHER

• • • •

GRIT

When someone is helping you over the hurdles, it may seem like they are being rough on you. Have the Grit to persevere, envision the result and move forward.

CHAPTER 12

THE ADVENTURE BEGINS

I'm on the right.

Leap of Faith

One year after my accident, I made the decision to go skydiving from 10,000 feet above sea level. I will never forget the pilot momentarily slowing down and saying, "You're getting off here!" My heartbeat shot way up as I realized we were definitely departing the aircraft. I instinctively resisted. There were three of us jumping that day. My friend had a camera attached to the top of his helmet to film the excursion, and I was strapped onto a harness with an instructor, a method called tandem jumping. We would jump together as one.

As we plunged toward Earth, I saw the plane to the left, the blue skies and Cape Canaveral off in the distance. For a little more than 41 seconds, we were birds in flight. As we were free-falling and zigzagging across the sky, I experienced total exhilaration and freedom. I phoned my parents that evening and said, with a great deal of emotion, "Hey there, Mom and Dad, guess what? I just jumped out of a perfectly good airplane from 10,000 feet!" There was a

moment of silence, then my dad said, "You did what?!"

Like my parents, you might wonder why I would do such a thing. It was not for the momentary thrill. I did it for the experience, for the chance to step outside of my comfort zone, my paralyzed state, and to stretch beyond my limitations. I wanted to do something markedly different, something most people would never do.

Actively seeking out different experiences opens your mind to new possibilities that can drive your personal and professional life forward. As I reflect on that skydiving experience, I am reminded of something Dr. Joyce Brothers said: "In each of us are places where we have never gone. Only by pressing the limits do we ever find them."

Lateral Thinking

Skydiving, even to this day, serves as a pleasant and effective reminder that we must step out of our paralyzed state by thinking laterally. The limitations we encounter, more often than not, are self-imposed. Once we bust through them, we realize that breaking away is not always such a bad thing.

Be Willing to Take That Leap

You never know what you can achieve until you take that leap. Do you want to be a manager or leader in your organization? Do you want to be the top sales producer? Do you want to be your own boss? How about a nurse, doctor, caregiver or a teacher? Do you want to be a stay-at-home dad and take care of your kids for a few years?

After I presented to one of the largest pharmaceutical companies in the world, I received an email indicating they'd started thinking laterally by putting my Vision, Mindset and Grit message into action: "Our goals for this Friday's conference call are to go over Vision – Best time to set up lunches with key offices; Mindset – Understanding our routing; Grit – Pushing through our ACS Triton studies."

I also presented to a Fortune 500 beverage company to show their teams why they should never rest on their laurels even if they continue to grow market share and retail space—and even if their customers love them. You need a clear Vision to know exactly what you are fighting for, I told them. It must be imprinted on your minds. You need the right Mindset to show up for work every day laser focused and on task, and you must constantly raise the bar—because your competition certainly is. And when you're ready to throw in the towel—or worse, maintain the status quo—you have to summon that Grit to push you forward.

When you put your Vision, Mindset and Grit into action in both your personal and professional life, these three simple yet powerful words can inspire you to reach above and beyond the expected. Do you want to travel the world with your family? In January 2010, the CEO of an international multilevel marketing company flew me around the world so I could deliver my most requested presentation, *Stand Up to Any Challenge*, to his company's conferences in San Francisco, the Gold Coast of Australia and Prague. It was a life-changing experience for me to see the world from so many different and enriching perspectives. That fantastic trip was possible only because I took a leap of faith to follow my dream of becoming a motivational speaker. I wanted to share my story and, in so doing, make a difference and enrich other people's lives.

Do you want to return to school and take a class? Do you want to save more money? Do you want to give back to your community? How about rising an hour earlier or attending a conference or trade show that is not mandatory? It all starts by simply brainstorming your desires, your dreams and where you want to be in the future. Thinking laterally, going for the out-of-the-ordinary experience, will enrich your life, stimulate your brain and open your mind to new possibilities.

Pivotal Moments in One's Life

When I returned home from Craig Hospital, life was very different. I was physically challenged and dependent upon my parents, but I kept my Vision clear. I wanted to return to college, get a degree and live a fulfilling life.

While recovering, I went to the gym and physical therapy three days a week and also enrolled at Indian River Community College. Six months later, my good friends, Bill and John Haas, Brendon McCarthy and John Salvador—guys I grew up with who were attending the University of Florida in Gainesville—thought it would be a good idea for me to move out of my parents' place and relocate to Gainesville, where they could look after me. I decided to go and transferred to Santa Fe Community College, the University of Florida's sister school. My goal was to earn my Associate Arts degree and eventually enroll in the University of Florida.

Life was good, my friends were great, I continued to work out, and I got stronger. I went back to FSU that year for a visit and, for the first time since the accident, saw Ed, the friend who had been driving the night of our accident. I told him I didn't blame him for what had happened, that we were both at fault, that I took responsibility for what had happened, and that I was okay. I had made peace and moved on. We exchanged numbers and promised to keep in touch.

Two years later, he called to tell me he was graduating from FSU and enrolling in the University of Florida to get his graduate degree. At FSU, we had both been members of Pi Kappa Alpha (Pikes) fraternity. He knew I had joined the same fraternity at the University of Florida and asked if I would mind if he did as well. I told him it was a great idea, thinking it would be an opportunity for us to renew our friendship.

After he enrolled, however, I felt little effort on his behalf. In the back of my mind, I accepted it. I could only imagine what I would have felt like if the shoe had been on the other foot.

On the way to a football game one Saturday night, we crossed paths. He was smoking cigars with a group of his friends. We made eye contact, then he quickly walked away. At that moment, I became intensely angry—at him, at myself, at my whole situation. My emotions ran wild. After the game, I went to a college bar where, for the first time ever, I drank to forget. When my friend Brendon McCarthy saw I was having a bad night, he refused to leave my side and safely drove me home. I couldn't even get out of the passenger side without his help. My legs were too weak to support me. Brendon hoisted me over his shoulders and carried me inside. "If I don't make it through this," I told him cryptically, "tell my parents, tell my mom, I love them."

The next morning, recalling the events of that evening— especially what I'd said to Brendon—terrified me. Not once since

I'd been diagnosed a quadriplegic had I ever had a single thought about suicide, yet that night, after seeing Ed, it suddenly crossed my mind. Why did bumping into him make me so upset, so angry inside that I actually considered doing something selfish? I mean, have you ever experienced something in your life that you believe has been unjust or unfair?

This is when I made the decision to once again let it happen. I let the anger move through me as opposed to defining me for the rest of my life. Easier said than done, yes, but trust me, it's possible. And so, with a year and a half of college still ahead, I decided to leave Gainesville—and the comfort and convenience of being close to some outstanding, wonderfully supportive friends—and start over yet again. This time on my own.

I ultimately graduated from the University of South Florida, in Tampa, and carved out a whole new life for myself. When I graduated, a friend, Steve Muro, a financial advisor for Northwestern Mutual, said, "Scott, if you want to turn lemons into lemonade, consider a career in the insurance and financial industry and specialize in disability insurance planning. Use your story to inspire others to consider protecting one of their most valuable assets—one's ability to earn an income." After that talk, I joined Northwestern Mutual as an agent, intent on using that platform to make a difference in people's financial lives.

This was a pivotal period in my own life. Difficult as it was leaving the comfort and security of my circle of friends, I knew I had to become more independent if I was ever going to extinguish the darkness and negativity I had been feeling. I had to become stronger in order to create a more positive outcome for myself.

As I reflect upon my life now, I realize that my decision then made all the difference. I took a risk, created a new Vision and persevered with a lot of Grit until I accomplished my goals. I haven't regretted it since.

VISION

Dream above and beyond the expected.

● ● ● ●

MINDSET

Think laterally.

● ● ● ●

GRIT

Once you step out of a plane, you are committed. There is no opportunity to turn back. Where in your life can you take that kind of leap of faith? Take that leap today and reap the rewards of a new experience. Grit will help you make the decision to take that leap, to try something entirely new.

CHAPTER 13

YOU GOTTA KEEP SWINGING

My journey to return to near normal came at a price. It took more than six years of my life, over 2,190 days and a tremendous amount of Grit to go to the simple use of a cane. During that time and countless hours of physical therapy, my strength improved to a point that I could grip and swing a golf club, maintain my balance and hit a golf ball. I was ecstatic!

Practice Makes Perfect

I had to make numerous adjustments to play. I had to learn to grip the golf club differently due to the weakness in my hands and fingers. Even though I can walk, my lower body behaves as though it is still paralyzed when I swing a golf club. I am unable to twist my lower body and

Playing the Plantation Golf Course at Kapalua, Maui (Hawaii), which ranks among the world's greatest.

utilize the strength needed to hit the ball and get good distance. Through trial and error, I found I could use more upper body strength to compensate for the loss of my lower body strength.

Making these adjustments and spending countless hours on the driving range hitting thousands of golf balls reignited my passion for the game. It is one thing to have had so much passion for a sport you loved to play and then have to say goodbye to it forever after being diagnosed a quadriplegic. It is quite another amazing thing to once again be able to play!

April Fools' Day

I will never in my life forget the day my dad challenged me to a round of golf on April 1, 2008, April Fools' Day. Believe it or not, I lost my balance, fell down and broke my lower left leg in two places. I bet you never thought golf could be such a hazard to your health. It takes courage to stand up again when you have been knocked down. Whether you are knocked down because of a failure in a relationship, a serious health issue, a financial setback or another difficulty, when you do stand up again you are stronger. It also builds character. It took me a full year of intense physical rehabilitation before I was able to get back on the golf course, but I did it.

I am reminded of the time I was in Puerto Rico, at the El Conquistador Resort, and decided to play a game on their beautiful golf course. I was paired with John, someone I didn't know. On our way to the first hole, he said, "Scott, why don't you have the honors and go first." I hobbled over to the first hole, bent down, put my tee in the ground and steadied the golf ball on it. I took my stance and aimed, then I heard that voice in my head saying, "Scott, now would be a great time for you to make an impression on your new golfing buddy."

Ever hear that voice in the back of your mind when you try to make a first impression with anyone?

Well, I figured if I could swing my club faster than I ever had before, that maybe, just maybe, my ball might go that much further. So, I took this monster swing. I swung so fast that the momentum knocked me onto the ground. So, there I was, facedown on the grass looking like a displaced beached whale.

The first thing I heard was John asking, "Scott, what in the world am I supposed to do now? Leave you?" To make matters even worse, as I turned my head around, I noticed my little white golf ball sitting firmly on the tee! So much for first impressions!

As we said our goodbyes, John turned to me and said, "I know you struggle while you walk, but what happened?" When I told him, he started to laugh. I said, "How can you be laughing at that?" He said, "I'm not laughing at you—I'm laughing with you. Do you know how difficult it's going to be for me to go home and tell my golfing buddies that a walking quadriplegic just beat me in a round of golf—by two shots!"

So, how did I really beat John? The same way you can beat your competition: focus more on your strengths than on your weaknesses. Focus on your industry knowledge, your expertise and what you believe separates you from your competition. And don't be afraid to make minor adjustments along the way when you're struggling to get the results you're shooting for.

Keep Swinging Toward Your Future

In life, you have to keep swinging!

I have learned that by challenging others to keep swinging they can change the direction of their lives. I will never forget the day I received an email from Dave Rusie. He said, "Hi, Scott. You probably don't remember me, but you spoke at a Jack Henry conference a couple of years ago and we talked afterward. I was inspired and related to you that I had lost my leg in a motorcycle accident while I was in college back in the 1960s. I loved golf, but had given up the game due to my prosthetic leg. After hearing you speak, I decided to take up the game I once loved and not let my physical handicap stop me."

He added, "Update 2012...I retired last fall from Jack Henry and have focused on many things since, but I did place an emphasis on golf. I bought a new set of clubs, took a few lessons and hit many thousands of balls on the practice range. I had not played a round of golf until I felt I would be comfortable, and I didn't want to burden fellow players. Those days of waiting are now behind me. My wife and I spent some time in your state of Florida this winter and golf was one of my top priorities (in addition to getting away from the winter cold in Indiana). I actually played well and beat a few people...As you know, that competitive spirit never goes away. Life is good...My golf game is back and for that I can only thank you for your inspirational talk."

In my opinion, a golf course mimics life. You have peaks and valleys, sand traps and water, and even the best of the female and male golfers struggle from time to time. Scores are kept to monitor your progress, and in the real world we call those goals, right? In

Golfing with Dad in Hawaii one year after I broke my leg.

a round of golf, you have a choice. You can compete with yourself or others, but we all know you are your own toughest competitor.

VISION

See complete success in your mind's eye first!

• • • •

MINDSET

Stand up when knocked down!

• • • •

GRIT

You gotta keep swinging!

CHAPTER 14

BE COACHABLE

I learned the importance of being coachable and emulating others at a very young age. Even today I am never shy about asking for help when I don't know something, whether it be in sports, business or my personal life. I have found it amazing what you can learn through other people's experiences if you simply ask. Surprisingly, I have never met anyone unwilling to talk about how they have succeeded. Their insights have created a value-added educational experience that continues to enrich my life, and they could have the same impact on yours.

Like so many people, my good friend Kris Venturini has had his own share of adversity in his personal and professional life. Through that adversity, he taught himself how to live and appreciate life in 30-minute increments. "You can only control the next 30 minutes," he says. "Learn to appreciate those moments, and you will begin to see things from a different perspective." Being coachable as well as open to new ideas, I tried implementing Kris' concept in my own life. Believe it or not, it works. Imagine what that thought process could do for you.

Some people have the mistaken notion that asking for help indicates weakness. It is as if not being able to handle a challenge on our own somehow makes us unworthy of it. I know I have reached many of my goals because I have asked for help along the way. I have conditioned myself with the Mindset that being coachable is essential to my eventual success.

In the midst of leading the Chicago Bulls to six world championships, NBA coach Phil Jackson was often asked about his superstar player Michael Jordan. Jackson said that many players in the league had the same physical skills as Michael Jordan. Many players, he also explained, had the dedication, the drive and even the Vision. The one trait separating Jordan from the many incredible league athletes, Jackson said, is that he is extremely coachable. "He listens intently to what I say. He accepts the input, then puts it into action." Jordan knew that on his own he could be good and even great. With the help of coaches, however, he could be spectacular.

After my accident, I returned to college to earn my Bachelor of Science degree in Finance, then joined Northwestern Mutual as an agent. One of the ways I was able to build a wonderful practice was by partnering with other successful agents, especially on complex cases. In addition, Al Granum, an agent with Northwestern Mutual, introduced Client Building and the One Card System, a proven track to success for financial service professionals. This system helped take my sales to the next level. Through my partnership with Lou Heckler, a top-tier speaking coach, I learned that by organizing and delivering my presentation differently, I could have more of a long-term impact on conference attendees. Jane Atkinson, a speaker coach and author of *The Wealthy Speaker,* helped me to accelerate my learning in order to catapult my speaking business.

We all can accelerate our progress, be more productive and achieve greater levels of expectations if we're willing to be coachable and partner with other people. That's why I love watching *Shark Tank*. The entrepreneurs pitching their ideas to Barbara Corcoran, Mark Cuban, Daymond John, Lori Greiner,

Robert Herjavec, Kevin O'Leary and others are looking to be coachable and partner with the best in hopes of taking their life and business to the next level. Remember, as I mentioned above, insights of others can create a value-added educational experience that can enrich your life as well as theirs.

Instant Replay

You always have the opportunity to take stock of your knowledge and skills. Have you ever analyzed how you handle certain situations? What could you do to improve upon your technique? I learned early on about the importance of watching yourself on film, whether or not you like what you are seeing.

As a wide receiver during a football play in high school, I was wide open to receive the ball. Our quarterback, Todd Laycock, tossed the ball back to our running back, Cleveland Gary, who would eventually play for the NFL. I was a good five steps in front of my defender, but for some reason I lost focus and the ball slipped between my arms for everyone to see. As my parents will tell you, they were first to proudly jump up to cheer me, and then quickly and quietly sat down wondering how in the world their boy dropped that pass.

The game had been filmed, and Coach Jones played that scene the next day, backward and forward, over and over again, right in front of the entire team—including good friends and star athletes such as Ronnie Kirchman, Victor Simmons, Mike Duhart, Dillon Murphy, Larry Eichhorn and Andy Pollard. It was painful to be there, with everybody watching and making light of the play, but I learned a great deal and was able to apply what I learned in future games. I also learned a lesson I carry with me today: It is important to review what you have been doing so you can improve what you are trying to accomplish, especially when it comes to realizing your next challenge.

Speaking of being coachable, I cannot help but share this note I received that Jeffrey Hiatt, from the Physician's Benefit Service, wrote to the meeting planner of the conference:

The final presentation from Scott was obviously inspirational. I anticipated this and had my family come to hear the presentation. Wow! Both of my daughters were moved, but especially my younger daughter, Melissa. After the speech, she went up to Scott to give him a big hug. The tears in her eyes brought tears not only to us, but to Scott. What a great story. At our kids' school, no writing, notes or other signs are allowed on the students' desks. Melissa had put Scott's message – "Vision, Mindset and Grit" on her desk. The teacher asked about it and, when Melissa explained what it meant to her, she was allowed to leave it up. Melissa had just begun to run in cross country. She was the smallest and youngest kid (6th grade) on the team, and we were hoping she could just finish the course. She ended up doing very well and was even beginning to beat the 8th graders. In the NH State Championship (all runners from all schools), Melissa was running against 275 girls in the 5th and 6th grades. Before the race we talked about 'Vision, Mindset and Grit.' Again, we hoped she would finish in the top 50. She blew the doors off of everyone. She came in first with 12 seconds between her and the 2nd place girl. Wow. The next day we began to get recruiting calls from the region's best running team. She has now run in the Boston "Mayor's Cup" Race and will be running in the regionals in Rhode Island in a few weeks. The purpose of this email is to thank you for helping to inspire my little girl to do her best. I believe the presentation by Scott helped to propel her to this victory.

VISION

Does your Vision allow you to be coachable? Is there room in your plan for the input of others who have something to teach you? Others' insights can propel you to new heights of success.

● ● ● ●

MINDSET

Use the concept of the Grip of Strategic Alignment to focus the Mindset of your team on working together to achieve a common goal.

● ● ● ●

GRIP & GRIT

Grip your team with a creative idea. Get a Grip on positivity and don't let go. Improve your Grip on the workings of your organization. Gripping is fundamental to success. Use Grit to master Grip.

CHAPTER 15

CONQUERING YOUR NEXT GREATEST CHALLENGE

A good friend of mine, whose name happens to be Brad Blessman, has been a blessing in my life. Brad believed in me the same way people in your life believe in you. He challenged me the same way you can challenge yourself to accomplish things you've wanted or needed to do or what others believe you cannot do. Blessman wanted to teach me to snow ski on my own from 12,000 feet above sea level up in the Rocky Mountains.

Now, I need to set the stage. The timing of this snow ski attempt was seven years after I walked out of Craig Hospital—a little over 2,190 days from my wheelchair to the use of forearm crutches, to using a simple walking cane, to an attempt to ski down the face of a mountain. I know what you are thinking. I am crazy, right? I would not call it crazy. I call it adventurous living!

Craig Hospital Revisited

I met Blessman in Denver, Colorado. During that time, I made it a point to visit Craig Hospital for the first time since I had walked out. Leslie, my physical therapist, Karen, my occupational therapist, and Dr. Luke were still there. It was a great reunion!

(left to right) Me, Mike Utley, my friend Jim Keckler.

Dr. Luke suggested I speak to a new patient, Mike Utley, who was the offensive lineman for the Detroit Lions. On November 17, 1991, in a game against the L.A. Rams, Mike had suffered an injury to his sixth and seventh cervical vertebrae, the same injury I had, and was diagnosed a quadriplegic. I was honored to meet him, and we had an amazing conversation. Before I left, I said, "You are entering the Super Bowl of your life. Keep the faith, focus on what you can control and never give up." One night, many years after we met, Mike was on TV. Two of his former Detroit Lions teammates were holding him up in parallel bars as he took a step! How is that for Grit!

Mountaintop Experience

Vail, Colorado, is among the most popular ski destinations in North America and throughout the world. Standing at the top of the mountain, I looked over the landscape; the terrain was awesome to behold. Magnificence was everywhere. As I peered down the mountain, I could see roads with tiny buses and cars making their way.

I recalled a sign posted at the base of the mountain. The message, probably written by an attorney with a sense of humor, in effect said, "If you are crazy enough to attach a pair of wooden planks to the bottom of your feet and take this lift to the top to ski a frozen mountain, then you are legally waiving all rights to a lawsuit in the event of injury."

I don't know about you, but this was not the confidence builder I had hoped for.

I was outfitted in a pair of forearm crutches

Brad Blessman (left) and me at 11,000 feet above sea level.

known as outriggers. The tips had one-foot snow skies attached to them. The outriggers had two functions: in the down position, they were designed to give support while standing and skiing; in the upright position, they acted as crutches—a pretty amazing piece of technology.

At the top of the mountain, I saw a shade of blue I never had seen before. Over the next day and a half I had fallen so often that that shade of blue turned black and blue and Advil became my best friend!

Breaking the Fall Line

At the end of the second day, Brad skied up and asked, "Do you know what you are doing wrong?" I replied, "No." Brad said, "You keep resisting what I am trying to teach you. If you want to learn how to ski, you have to be willing to lean forward, break the fall line and let gravity help you down the mountain." Easier said than done, I assure you. I could not do it for the life of me. It was too steep and I was scared.

Apparently, many people resist this experience when learning to snow ski. Who wants to fall? Who wants to fail? Yet, failure may give you the best opportunity to master something new, to break the fall line and view all your challenges from an entirely different perspective.

At the end of the second day, I was exhausted and sore physically, mentally and emotionally. Even so, I decided to give it another effort. I convinced myself this was nothing more than going the extra mile, pushing that extra one-eighth of an inch.

Zigging and Zagging

Listening to what Brad was teaching me, I leaned forward and held my breath as I broke the fall line. Believe it or not, with every last ounce of Grit I could muster and under Brad's coaching, I found myself skiing in the upright position on my own and in full control. Zigzagging, I stopped a few hundred yards later, standing upright. It was surreal! When Brad skied down to give me a high five, he noticed I was pretty teary-eyed.

I explained to him, "I just experienced a sensation I thought I had lost forever on the beach the night before my accident. I experienced the sensation of what it was like to run again, and I found a whole new passion in my life." Helen Keller once said, "Life is either a daring adventure or nothing at all."

When you find that kind of passion in both your personal and professional life, you will surely find your drive to stand up and break the fall line when it comes to overcoming your challenges and taking advantage of opportunities by using the three essential tools: Vision, Mindset and Grit!

China Bowl at 12,000 Feet

On the sixth and last day, Brad took me back up to the top of Vail. We then we traversed from one mountaintop to the next until we came to a ledge just under 12,000 feet above sea level, overlooking a massive crater on the back side of the mountain. It's called China Bowl, a double black diamond ski run with the most difficult terrain. I had only been skiing for six days! I paused for a moment to take it all in. "Blessman," I said, "I'm curious. Where is the lift to take us back down?" "There isn't one," he said. "The only way back is down China Bowl." Obviously seeing my mild panic, he said, "Don't be afraid. I'll ski right behind you like I have been and will pick you up when you fall."

As you might imagine, a lot of scenarios were running through my mind. It had been seven years since I was told I would never walk again, and here I was about to ski down a mountain.

I was both excited and terrified. The run was steep. How I felt in that moment reminds me of the poet David Whyte, who wrote, "The price of our vitality is the sum of all our fears. Vitality means to grow, to survive." So, if you want to continue to grow and survive, both personally and professionally, you need to be fearless and unafraid to break the fall line in your life.

All kinds of fears surfaced within me: fear of failure, fear of letting Brad down, of not meeting my own expectations and, of course, the most obvious fear of falling down and reinjuring myself. Nevertheless, something within told me to proceed. I felt

I would tap into my true potential in spite of my circumstances and give every last drop of Grit.

There I was, a person who had trouble walking on flat land at sea level, ready to navigate mountain terrain. I trusted Brad and had a new level of trust in my own abilities. I knew to bend my knees, square my shoulders, transfer my weight and break the fall line. It was time to go for it on my own two feet. No more observations, no more recollections. Then I heard Brad yell out, "Let's go!"

Skiing down China Bowl was one of the most difficult things I had done since becoming paralyzed and walking again. When I fell—and I fell a lot—Brad was right there to hoist me up. I was way too weak from my paralysis to do it on my own. For a long time it seemed I was hurtling along at a furious pace toward some distant and future target, and then I would fall. Blessman picked me up. Then I would fall again and again.

Someone who skies those types of double black diamond runs can get down the mountain quickly. It took me over 45 minutes. When we arrived at the bottom, standing together, we both collapsed on the ground, completely exhausted! Looking up to where we had just come from, we saw tiny dots of people making their way down. Brad said, "Look up, Scotty. You accomplished something that most skiers never do because they're scared to ski these types of difficult runs, but you did it."

When we were halfway down China Bowl, I had fallen again. We rested for a few minutes longer than usual. Brad said he actually was hoping I would say I was too tired to go any farther because he was so winded and exhausted from picking me up. He said, "That's when I wanted to find a ski patrol to help me get you down the mountain on a stretcher. But then I thought, how in the world can I quit in front of you if you're unwilling to quit yourself?"

Such Great Heights

On that day, years after being paralyzed from my chest down and having been told I would never walk again, I crossed the finish line with my friend, Brad Blessman. Five years later, I had built up enough strength in my arms to pick myself up on the slopes without needing assistance. It was then I became an independent

skier, free to ski some of the most difficult runs in North America by myself.

Standing on top of a mountain 12,000 feet above sea level gives you a fantastic view of your next destination. Getting to your next destination, though, you need to have the Right Mindset, a Tenacious Vision, Tremendous Grit and a Blessman in your life. Who is the "Blessman" pushing you to your limits and stretching you above any of your own self-perceived, paralyzing limitations? More importantly, to whom are you being a "Blessman"? Whose life can you change today, tomorrow and the next day? After all, isn't that what life is all about? Making a difference in other people's lives?

Giving Back of Oneself

Brad reached out to help someone. He will tell you the experience had an incredible impact on his life. Brad put me in a position that gave me back my running legs unexpectedly, an experience I will never forget.

My run down China Bowl was one of my grandest experiences thus far, perhaps second only to walking out of Craig Hospital. More experiences will come. When you are willing to raise your game and face different types of challenges or obstacles and find yourself hesitant to depart from the familiar and cozy confines of your self-imposed paralyzed state, look back to your grandest experiences or borrow one of mine and make the commitment to press forward. Take action to seize an opportunity that can open up the door of confidence. You have to dig deep and pull up from within to persevere. This is pure Grit! Mae West once said, "You only live once, but if you do it right once is enough."

Celebrate your successes, then reset new goals once you've reached each goal. Continuously adapt, be flexible and make adjustments along the way until each goal has been met. Creating new goals in your life fuels the fire of inspiration. Don't be afraid to break the fall line in your life.

I'm leaning forward and demonstrating to 500 sales reps why Breaking the Fall Line and Going with What Scares You can separate you from the competition and help you get to your next destination!

VISION

Focus on your Vision, develop the Mindset
to realize it and recognize taking risks
will likely be a part of the journey.

● ● ● ●

MINDSET

Do you have a systematic plan like Vision, Mindset
and Grit to improve your effectiveness?

● ● ● ●

GRIT

Sometimes taking a step back and reflecting how
far you have come helps gain perspective.

CHAPTER 16

GO ABOVE AND BEYOND THE EXPECTED

Fire Walk

One year before I gave my first speech, I attended a seminar by noted self-help author and motivational speaker Tony Robbins. What an amazing experience. During his seminar, Tony prepared everyone to focus in ways we had never focused before. We focused so intensely that we were able to "Fire Walk"—walk over hot coals without getting burned. Tony instilled in us the focus and confidence we needed to walk 10 to 15 feet barefoot over hot coals. Yes, I and more than 2,000 people did this successfully!

Through fire walking, Tony Robbins gets everyone believing what they can do. This, in turn, gets people believing they can achieve the impossible—if only they believe they can. Amazing! Changing the way we do things, what we think, what we believe we can accomplish, can be scary, inspiring and rewarding all at the same time.

Even if you're not in sales, I think you'll relate to the following. One of the most difficult and scary things for people in the sales world is to ask for referrals from their clients. For whatever reason, they are afraid to ask, perhaps because of the fear of being rejected. That is what I experienced. However, that changed after cold calling for two years, building my insurance practice. It changed after a joke I heard. "Do you know the difference between cold calling and referrals? Cold calling is God's punishment for not asking for referrals!"

In my fifth year with Northwestern Mutual, with the help of referrals and partnering with other agents on complex cases, and using Al Granum's Client Building and One Card System, I qualified for the Million Dollar Round Table, a 100% commission-driven reward that fewer than 8% of my peers from around the world—representing 500 companies in 70 countries—achieve on a yearly basis.

A Galaxy of Stars

The 1994 Million Dollar Round Table conference was held in Dallas, Texas. I encountered top producers in every direction I looked. I realized that as well as I was doing, there would be more to learn and room for more growth. Like a newly elected senator walking the halls of Congress for the first time, as I looked around I realized some people had been there for many years. I envisioned reaching the next level designation, based on commissions, called "Top of the Table" and one day reaching the ultimate "Court of the Table."

Returning from the Million Dollar Round Table event, I was involved in a minor car accident with major consequences. A motorist to my left accidentally ran a stop sign, caught me off guard, and we collided. We were both wearing seat belts. The police report indicated the other driver was at fault and was not hurt, but I was. I had injured the ulnar nerve in my right elbow, which controls the strength in the pinky and ring finger. It is the only hand I can use to grip my cane firmly to walk. My left hand is still way too weak as a result of my ongoing paralysis.

With the additional damage to the ulnar nerve came unexpected complications that would affect the grip in my right hand. Long story short, I had surgery, and afterward the strength in my hand did not return. Walking with a cane 90% of the time as an outside salesman now posed certain risks—like the risk of losing my grip and unexpectedly falling down and injuring myself.

It was suggested by someone in the insurance industry that I consider reintroducing a wheelchair into my life. Having fought so hard to get out of a wheelchair, the last thing I wanted to do was to use one again. Over the next few months, I struggled mentally and emotionally. That is when I made the difficult decision to walk away from a successful business and industry for which I had so much passion.

So, how did I turn this setback onto a comeback? The martial arts teach that when you're being attacked your opponent will sometimes drop their guard. That can be your golden opportunity to strike back—to deliver your counterpunch. The same is true in real life. Today, some of you are experiencing daunting challenges and not making significant headway. Be patient and wait for the opportunity to deliver your own knockout counterpunch. However, if it doesn't come—and it may not—know that you can still discover the silver lining within ANY adversity. That silver lining is the lesson learned that may have a far greater impact along your life's journey.

In these moments, we must believe that things happen for a reason and that we can turn setbacks into comebacks. My counterpunch converted my new challenge into success.

Exporting You-Know-What...

I went back on the offensive, looking forward to the next chapter in my life. I kept an open mind and was determined to find investment opportunities in unfamiliar landscapes. That is when my brother, Mark, approached me with a global idea utilizing golf course contacts he had in Hong Kong and Singapore. At the time, Mark was an outside salesman promoting and selling fertilizer to golf courses in his home state of Florida. To keep up with the ongoing changes in his industry and stay ahead of his competition, he was expanding his perspective. After reviewing his business and marketing plan, and after much deliberation, I saw an investment opportunity he desperately needed and decided to take a significant financial risk.

Mark's out-of-the-box idea was to partner with manufacturers in Florida who had the ability to custom-blend fertilizers, then export them directly to golf courses in Southeast Asia. His competition in Asia had found custom-blending to be too expensive or impractical. Mark was able to make it work, however, and in doing so created a niche market. His company was soon exporting 40-foot containers loaded with fertilizer—in some cases in excess of 28 U.S. tons per container. By maximizing the container space and weight, his company could offer better pricing while maintaining high-quality product and fantastic service. Mark went one step further. He realized he could also export hazardous and nonhazardous golf course chemicals into those fertilizer containers and offer the same products to his clients at a lower cost, maximizing a new revenue stream.

Basically, I suppose you could say this company exports *you-know-what* to China!

After the first fiscal year, Mark's company generated sales in excess of $1.3 million. He was dreaming in Full Color and traveling overseas to Hong Kong, Malaysia, Singapore, Taiwan and Indonesia, building relationships with golf course superintendents and prospective distributors.

Interestingly, my dad had also been doing business throughout Asia. Years prior, he retired as a golf course superintendent and became a consulting agronomist—essentially, a soil doctor. He, too, grew his new business both nationally and internationally. He was a tremendous advocate for my brother, as you might imagine.

Global Mindset

What I continue to learn today from this international experience is the strength behind creating a global mindset, a mindset that gets you thinking bigger on your own behalf, your organization's behalf and those you serve. Scaling your efforts, blending cultures, embracing diversity and your willingness to partner with people can create unforeseen opportunities that can expand possibilities. When you are expanding, you are growing; when you are growing, you are changing; when you are changing, your Vision, Mindset and Grit strengthen.

Capitalizing on Diversity

Today, like it or not, we live in a global economy with competition all over the world. Increased globalization may require more interaction among people from different cultures and backgrounds. You may have noticed increased diversity in the workforce. In a sense, diversity is accepting, understanding and valuing differences among people in all walks of life around the world regardless of where you live. For this reason alone, we must be open to change, welcome inclusion and take the time to understand we can all benefit if we are willing to understand each other and strive to work together. Embracing diversity can stimulate creative thinking and innovation across an organization and drive success. Just like Lululemon's success, which is evident and something we can learn from. Their philosophy is "As a design-led company, curiosity is at our core. We're constantly thinking about how we can innovate our process, our gear and our social impact so we can elevate the world from mediocrity to greatness."

The Risk–Reward Relationship

Learning how to rethink outside the box, dream in Full Color and take meaningful, calculated and informed risks can give you the competitive advantage in any area of your life. As an investor in my brother's idea, I witnessed many mistakes the company made as it strived to grow internationally while coping with currency fluctuations, the roller coaster of commodity prices, as well as ocean freight and Asian distributors wanting bigger commissions. However, when you are stretching, taking action, making mistakes and failing, you are living, growing and learning. Take advantage and look to your own failures and mistakes as opportunities for both personal and professional growth. Giacomo Casanova said, "One who makes no mistakes makes nothing at all."

While I was an agent with Northwestern Mutual Life between 1989 and 1994, I had the privilege of watching many motivational speakers at their annual conference in Milwaukee, Wisconsin— speakers such as Terry Bradshaw, the famous Pittsburgh Steelers quarterback, and Charlie Plumb. Charlie graduated from the Naval Academy at Annapolis and went on to fly the F-4 Phantom jet on 74 successful missions over Vietnam. On his 75th mission, with only five days before he was to return home, Charlie was shot down, captured, tortured and imprisoned in an 8' x 8' cell. He spent the next 2,103 days as a POW in communist prisons.

What really resonated with me was how Charlie told his story of overcoming adversity and how he drew parallels between his POW experience and the challenges of everyday personal and professional life. I walked away thinking about my own life, how far I had come, the choices I had made and the challenges I was trying to conquer. From that day forward, a seed was planted in my mind: I wanted to be like Plumb, a motivational speaker, and share my story with the world

It wasn't until 2002, after getting married, that I pursued that dream. My first few speeches were at local Rotary Clubs, hospitals and human resource meetings in Tampa, Florida, where my wife and I resided. My first corporate speech took place almost two years later. My cousin, Doug Greenwell, a top-producing financial representative for Country Financial, helped arrange for me to speak at his company's upcoming annual sales conference in Springfield, Illinois. It was an amazing experience.

When I returned to Tampa, I received a phone call from a representative from Investacorp. His wife had heard me speak at a recent human resource meeting and thought I would be a

(left to right) John Salvador, his daughters Jordan and Haley, me, and John's wife, Carolyn.

good candidate for their upcoming conference in Beaver Creek, Colorado. I was ecstatic for the opportunity!

Returning from that engagement, my good friend, John Salvador, and his wife, Carolyn, introduced me to a human resource business partner for a multimillion-dollar national food service company, US Foods. He arranged for me to speak to their Atlanta sales division. It was a terrific experience and generated referrals. Over the next few years, 15 other sales divisions asked me to kick off their conferences from coast to coast.

Corporations were taking notice and, with my wife's encouragement, my dream was becoming reality. I was now giving back to humanity in ways I had always wanted to after seeing Charlie Plumb speak. To this day, speaking is great therapy for me. Reliving my life-changing experience allows me to give back and make a difference in people's lives. In turn, I feel my life is enriched.

I've shared the stage with such luminaries as Rudy Giuliani and the late Stephen Covey, as well as Olympic gold medalists Bonnie Blair and Jackie Joyner-Kersee, to name a few.

Speaking allowed my wife and me to travel across the U.S., as well as throughout the world. We met some amazing people on our journeys and had a lot of fun along the way. We visited many famous sites, including the Taj Mahal in India, the Great Barrier Reef, Sydney Harbor, Ayers Rock and the world-famous Sydney Opera House in Australia. We toured the Parthenon in Athens, Greece, the Roman Coliseum and Vatican City in Italy. In Mexico, we saw the Chichen Itza, the Mayan City and pyramids. In Canada, we toured Banff, a beautiful ski resort, and Lake Louise, with a beautiful glacier sitting on top of a mountain. On a night flight to Edmonton, Canada, we watched the Northern

Lights dazzle the sky for over an hour. In Hong Kong, we visited the Big Buddha, known as Tian Tan Buddha, located on Lantau Island. In Prague, we walked over the famous Charles Bridge, one of the most romantic sites in that beautiful city, and toured Prague Castle, the largest complex of its kind in the world.

Unfortunately, our marriage came to an end in 2011. It was a very difficult period for both of us—and one of the most trying times of my life other than being diagnosed a quadriplegic. During that time, I almost lost my life again. In May of 2011, I was experiencing severe chest pain. Climbing the stairs in our house, I became short of breath. I didn't understand what was wrong. I just assumed the chest pain was the result of stress from going through the divorce.

I waited nine days before going to the emergency room. An EKG turned out to be negative—a good sign. Then a dye was injected into my bloodstream. The doctors found four clots lodged in my right lung and one in my left. An ultrasound further revealed a large clot in my right calf, part of which had broken off. These smaller clots were moving and pressing toward the outer wall of my lungs. I was put on morphine for the pain and given heparin, a blood thinner, to dissolve the clots. For the next seven days, I lay in intensive care, knowing that my next breath could be my last. It was 27 years since I had been diagnosed a quadriplegic, and once again I was reliving a nightmare that might take my life.

One of the doctors commented that it was amazing I was alive considering how long I had waited to go to the hospital. Knowing he was right, I prayed and made my peace with God. I would fight to stay alive—and mentally, I would welcome life thereafter. I have lived a good life. I would not change my experience for the world. If you could see the world through my eyes and experience what I have, you would understand.

With tremendous support from family and friends, I survived 2011 medically and emotionally. I've learned that life is full of peaks and valleys, and how we choose to respond to these challenges determines whether or not we will prevail.

(l-r) Me, Mom, my brother Mark and his wife, Dawn, my stepmom, Susan, my dad, my sister, Heidi. (front) My brother's daughter, my niece, Samantha.

Back in 1998 through 2002, I took a big risk and tried something new as an investor. I was intrigued with short-term investing in the stock market, called day trading—buying and selling stocks over the course of a day, attempting to maximize investment returns whether the market goes up or down. Once I understood the concept, my investment returns far exceeded my expectations. One year I made over $250,000 in capital gain profits.

In 2001, however, things changed. I lost my focus and struggled. This was not only happening to me; it was happening to other people I knew who were also day trading. The investment strategies we had been using just stopped working. Daily profits quickly turned into daily losses.

Looking back, the problem was that instead of adjusting to a changing market, I stayed with what had worked for me in the past. That stagnation cost me dearly. I was now giving back a lot of investment income I had earned. Over the next year, I struggled with the idea that I was failing miserably at day trading. Failing at anything is not the best feeling in the world, but it is an opportunity to learn more about yourself—if you allow that learning to take place.

I took the failure with stride, walked away from day trading and learned something of great value: If you are unwilling to make adjustments and adapt to a changing world, you will fall behind. Take notice when things are not going as planned. Make adjustments. Embrace change—and be willing to create change to help you stay ahead.

I lost my focus and, in my mind, I had failed. But if you're unwilling to experience failure in life, how else can you expect to learn to become stronger?

VISION

Be creative.

● ● ● ●

MINDSET

Always room for more growth.

● ● ● ●

GRIT

Never give up hope.

CHAPTER 17

THINK OUTSIDE THE BOX

Bike, Bath and Boating

What gives you that creative boost? For me, it has everything to do with the three B's: Bike, Bath and Boating. I love doing 15-mile bike rides three times a week, taking long baths to soak my quadriplegic bones, and boat rides. My three-wheeled bike is hand-cranked and designed for individuals with permanent, physical, lower-limb impairment or those who cannot use their lower extremities very well. Today, handcycling is also a Paralympic sport. A dear friend, Oz Sanchez, won gold and bronze medals in this sport at both the 2008 Beijing Paralympics and 2012 London Paralympics.

It's during my long bike rides, hot baths and boating that my mind wanders. That is where I come up with my most creative ideas. What is your bike, bath and boat? What do you enjoy doing a few times a week by yourself that can inspire your creative vision?

On a long bike ride a few years back, I realized that outside-the-box thinking is what brings real change to our lives. I have learned that being open to creating change in your life, as opposed to sitting back and waiting for change to happen, can fuel new passions. As you know, I love golf. That passion inspired me to take a risk and team up with my brother, Mark. What is your golf club? What hobby do you enjoy doing that can inspire a new idea you could use tomorrow to change your life?

Cane Man Coming Through

I learned something new from an experience I had that caught me off guard. It was New Year's Eve on Bourbon Street. I was with friends in New Orleans while attending the Nokia Sugar Bowl to watch the University of Florida and Florida State football teams battle it out. Around 12:30 a.m. on New Year's morning, after taking in New Year's Eve at Pat O'Brien's just off Bourbon Street, my legs were getting tired, so I grabbed my cane, said my goodbyes to friends who wanted to keep celebrating and headed back to the hotel. The streets were flooded with people, shoulder to shoulder. I was right in the middle of it. The crowd shifted hard to the right, then to the left, then back again to the right. I lost my balance and fell down.

The problem was that the crowd kept shifting and, without knowing it, people were now actually stepping on me. I was helpless. In that moment, a gentleman about 6-foot-4 and 300 pounds reached down and said, "Hey, you down there, Happy New Year! My name is Leroy, I am 41 years old, born and raised in New Orleans, and it looks like you can use a hand up." As he hoisted me up, he said, "Where are you headed?"

"To the end of Bourbon Street," I replied.

"I'm headed in the same direction," he said. "Why don't you follow me? I'll make a hole. Stay close behind me." Then he started yelling out seven words over and over again with a tremendous amount of passion: "Watch out people, handicap man coming through."

He not only made a hole, he parted the Red Sea!

Over and over again, he continued to repeat the mantra. Those ahead who did not listen were grabbed ever so gently as Leroy pointed to me and said, "See, that's handicap man." This continued for two blocks and, while we were making great progress, I was quite embarrassed. At that point, Leroy was not looking back to see if I was behind him, so I simply stepped to the right, stopped and watched him continue his march yelling, "Handicap man coming through!"

About ten minutes later, Leroy tracked me down and said, "What happened to you? I was worried!"

Quick on my feet, I said, "Leroy, you were walking way too fast for me."

"No worries. I'll slow it down."

I didn't know what to say, but replied, "Okay, sounds good to me. In the meantime, can you stop yelling *handicap man coming through*?"

Without missing a beat, he said, "Scott, does that bother you?"

"No, I just don't like the way you are presenting it!" I replied.

"No worries. Are you ready to go?" At that moment Leroy started yelling out "Cane man coming through" over and over with a tremendous amount of enthusiasm.

Adapt on the Fly

Humor, laughter and fun can get you through the most difficult challenges and to your destination! Remember, laughing is our saving grace. I would like to point out that Leroy did not know me, but he saw a man down and he helped me up. He then asked a question. I answered, he listened, and I followed.

As you may have gathered, I was not thrilled with the way he was communicating, so I bailed. However, when Leroy went searching and found me ten minutes later, he asked a question, I answered, he listened, and in a moment's notice he adapted on the fly. Leroy made an adjustment in his approach. I followed him again, and we both got to our destination.

I think you will find a tremendous amount of value in how Leroy responded to the situation. If you think about it, you will draw the same conclusion about what Leslie and my dad said as well. There is great value in adapting on the fly, value in being flexible and value in *letting it happen*. If you think about where you were yesterday and what it took you to get to where you are today, you'll begin to understand the importance of flexibility. If you are going to reach your next destination, you will have to be willing to adapt, to be flexible and maybe to *let it happen*. Never forget your Vision and those things you are fighting for, because we are living in a world that is accelerating. You are either preparing yourself to keep up or you will be left behind.

The ability to adapt in life is one thing, but the ability to adapt on the fly is quite another. Adapting on the fly can help you navigate through your own "Bourbon Street" challenges successfully.

VISION

Create a compelling Vision—
one that entices you to take action.

• • • •

MINDSET

Be willing to adapt on the fly.

• • • •

GRIT

Believe you will reach your
destination regardless of circumstances.

CHAPTER 18

BE INSPIRED

had long wanted to be a motivational speaker. Back in 1989, I was referred to Art Berg, who had become a widely sought-after speaker in the late 1990s. His client list read like the Fortune 500. Art went on to become a stellar success in business, in wheelchair sports and in life. In the early '90s, he completed a 325-mile wheelchair marathon. He was just amazing. It took him nine days to finish the race. When a reporter asked why he did it, Art's response was, "To prove that limits can be exceeded, barriers can be broken and that no circumstances can ever override the power of the human spirit!"

I reached out to Art to see if we could partner. He sent me some great information to get started. Several years later, when I called him, one of his staff members told me Art had passed away three months earlier from a toxic reaction to a prescription drug. He died the same month his book, *The Impossible Just Takes a Little Longer,* had been published by HarperCollins. He left behind his wife and three children. Art was a young 39 years old.

Invictus

Art named his company Invictus Communications. *Invictus* is a Latin word meaning *unconquered* or *invincible*. *Invictus* is also a poem that Art recited to the Baltimore Ravens football team when they hired him one season to be their motivational guru. The Ravens went on to win the Super Bowl that year. For his inspiring efforts, Art was given one of the Super Bowl rings, and the owner of the team had the word *Invictus* displayed on the jumbo screen after the win.

Art learned of the word *Invictus* from an 18th century poet, William Ernest Henley. When Henley was 24 years old, one of his legs was amputated below the knee as the result of complications from tuberculosis. They told him they had to amputate his other leg or he would die, but he refused. Instead, he persevered and, remarkably, walked out of the hospital some 21 months later never to return. During his stay in the hospital, he wrote the now famous poem, *Invictus*.

Out of the night that covers me,
Black as the Pit from pole to pole,
I thank whatever gods may be
For my unconquerable soul.
In the fell clutch of circumstance
I have not winced nor cried aloud.
Under the bludgeonings of chance
My head is bloody, but unbowed.
Beyond this place of wrath and tears
Looms but the Horror of the shade,
And yet the menace of the years
Finds, and shall find, me unafraid.
It matters not how strait the gate,
How charged with punishments the scroll.
I am the master of my fate:
I am the captain of my soul.

I Am the Captain of My Soul

Today, before I appear on stage, during my introduction I play an opening video that shows me kickboxing and knocking out my opponent. Then the screen goes black and the word Vision appears with two loud heartbeats. As that fades, the word Mindset appears with two loud heartbeats. As that fades, the word Grit appears with two loud heartbeats. When that disappears, a series of photographs of my accident appears, showing me lying on a stretcher and being lifted into an air ambulance. A progression of accident pictures follows, giving the audience a visual of what happened to me right after the terrible event. As they view the pictures, you hear my recorded voice reciting the poem *Invictus*.

It is my tribute to Art Berg.

Invictus is powerful, and I know the poem has an impact on many lives. A few years ago I received a note from an individual who heard me speak at the Seminole Cooperative conference. He said, "I have noticed that I was repeating the sentence 'I am the captain of my soul' to myself a couple times during the past week. It helped me increase my confidence; it made me realize that I am in control of my life; it gave me hope and belief in taking charge of my life at work and home; and it made a tremendous impact on me."

Stand Up to Your Challenges

I learned early in life, and have relearned many times since, that the quality of our lives is determined by the choices we make and by focusing on those things we can control. That's why I'm inspired by author J.K. Rowling, who said, "It is our choices, that show what we truly are, far more than our abilities." The challenges I have faced throughout my life, both personal and professional—some I willingly took on and some that were cast upon me—have helped me to grow and learn in ways that likely would not have otherwise happened. It is my hope that my story and insights will do the same for you and others.

> *Vision, Mindset and Grit, articulated in its most simple form, can help you achieve your dreams, your goals and your aspirations, both personally and professionally, and can turn impossibilities into possibilities. All you have to do is take action!*

VISION

Limits can be exceeded if you believe they can.

• • • •

MINDSET

I am the Master of my Fate.
I am the Captain of my Soul.

• • • •

GRIT

Take action.

CHAPTER 19

GUIDING LIGHTS

As I mentioned earlier, the divorce I went through left me paralyzed. What's ironic is that I conquered physical paralysis but found myself struggling with emotional paralysis. During that turmoil, my dad said to me: "Scott, a few years ago you gave me a DVD of you speaking to a group. Do you remember?" "Yes, sir," I said. "I suggest you do yourself a favor," he continued. "Watch it, then start practicing what you preach."

Don't you hate that! Someone offering you your own advice? Turns out it was some of the best advice I've ever received, though.

By applying the principles of Vision, Mindset and Grit over the next two years, my life changed dramatically. I managed to break free of being emotionally paralyzed, my divorce became final, my speaking business more than doubled, I started working out and lost 15 pounds, I wrote this book, and I decided to attend my 30th high school reunion, which I was reluctant to do as a single man. At that reunion, I had a wonderful conversation with Kim, a former classmate. There were about 600 people in our graduating class, and Kim and I didn't run in the same circles. Our conversation that night continued beyond the reunion, and she became the love of my life. On March 18, 2016, I took her snow skiing in Vail, Colorado. On a ledge at just under 12,000

Kim and me

feet above sea level, overlooking China Bowl, I proposed—and Kim said yes… :-)

I never met someone like Kim or anyone who makes me feel the way she does. Behind those green eyes, she has a beautiful heart and a sensitive, nurturing soul. She also has three amazing kids—Alexandra, Samantha and Gregory—who are now part of my life.

Kim had the opportunity to meet my dad before he passed away surrounded by family, on August 15, 2015, after losing his battle to cancer. Before Dad died, I told him that as long as I continued to speak I would have the privilege to carry his legacy forward, and for that I would be eternally grateful. Since then, during all of my book signings, I have added the phrase Dad whispered to me that helped me through my darkest hours: "Let it happen."

Just finished riding ATVs in Mexico: Me, Kim, Gregory, Samantha, Alexandra.

After the funeral, I flew to Fort Worth, Texas, to kick off three conferences I knew would be emotionally difficult for me. During this most challenging time, various events occurred within days of each other—one was a dream of a younger version of my dad. As I woke up remembering my dream of him walking up to me, nodding with a smile and holding up his hand showcasing the okay sign. I knew at that point that, once again, he was telling me that everything was going to be okay. That same day, I was moved by the site of a bronze Mexican statue by artist Jorge Martin called the Wings of the City and felt that I knew my dad was now my guardian angel.

Then, early that Saturday morning, I received a phone call from Ed, my friend who was driving during the accident that left me paralyzed in 1984. He told me a good friend of his was biking and hit a pothole, sending him over the handlebars. Although he was wearing a helmet at the time, he broke his neck and had a serious spinal cord injury that left him paralyzed from the chest down and diagnosed a quadriplegic— just like had happened to me. I expressed my sympathy and

Days after my dad passed, I saw these wings in Houston...Heaven!

asked how I could help. Ed said, "I don't have the courage to go see him, just like I did not have the courage to see you. Could you could help me through this?" "Yes, of course," I said. "Ed, you have to let go of the past as I have. Your friend needs you as much as you need him. Encourage him to fight the fight of his life, knowing that if he does, perhaps, like me, he will go the distance, too."

A few days later, Ed told me that he indeed went to see his friend and that it was a good experience for both of them. He also asked if I wouldn't mind sending his friend one of my books. "Absolutely!" I said.

EPILOGUE

FULL CIRCLE

One afternoon, I encountered Ivy, a longtime friend, who was a meeting planner in Tampa at the time. I told her I was interested in becoming a motivational speaker. She mentioned she had attended a conference at the Hyatt in Beaver Creek, Colorado. During that conference, she said she had heard the most captivating speaker, Art Berg.

Destiny, Perhaps

A year after that experience, a company named Investacorp invited me to be the keynote motivational speaker to an audience of more than 200 financial advisors at their annual company retreat held at the Hyatt in Beaver Creek, Colorado. This beautiful resort rests at the base of the mountain in the same location my friend, the meeting planner from Tampa, had seen Art Berg present.

I felt childlike excitement, but I was also profoundly nervous. I had invited my friend, Brad Blessman, who lives in Denver, and his father, Lyle, a former president of the Million Dollar Round Table, to attend my presentation that day. Thoughts swirled through my head. Beaver Creek is right next door to Vail, Colorado, the same place Blessman had taught me how to snow ski on my own two feet a mere seven years after I had walked out of Craig Hospital. Sitting in my wheelchair before I went on stage, I watched my opening video from the sidelines. It contained the series of pictures I mentioned from the accident and my recorded recitation of *Invictus* over those pictures.

Here I was about to present where Art had presented. The Blessmans were in the audience sitting next to the president of Investacorp. As I heard my own voice recite the poem Art had shared with so many groups and the Super Bowl-winning Baltimore Ravens, I felt overcome with emotion. I smiled, said a prayer and thought to myself, "Is this destiny or what!" Emotions were running at an all-time high. Lyle told me if I had delivered that same address to the Million Dollar Round Table, I would have won the hearts of thousands of agents.

St. George Island Revisited

In 2006, 22 years after my accident, I presented to a group near Panama City, Florida. After the presentation, I drove to St. George Island, the place where my life had changed forever. Ironically, the beach road and the dunes had changed little since November 3, 1984. I drove to the location where we most likely had camped on that fateful night. I walked on the beach, remembering my last sprint in the sand. It seemed like centuries had passed since the accident—yet, at the same time, it felt like only yesterday. Here I was, standing on the very spot along my life's path that led me to become the man I am today.

I thought about Ed and wondered what had happened to him. The last time we saw each other was two years after the accident when we made eye contact at that college football game. I remembered the anger I felt running through my veins that night and the drinking I did afterward to try to help me forget. I realized that Ed must have struggled, too, in ways many could never imagine. The tough part for me, though—and it *was* tough—was being in the hospital and physical rehab for six months without Ed ever coming to see me. He didn't call or write either.

Before putting the finishing touches on this book, I sought him out on Facebook—and friended him! A few days later, he accepted and sent along a message. Paraphrased, he said, "Scott, it's so good to hear from you. Not a day goes by that I don't think about St. George Island. Two lives were changed forever that night. I wish I could go back and alter what happened because I have been riddled with remorse and guilt ever since."

Ease his pain, I thought. Those are the same words Kevin Costner heard in the movie *Field of Dreams*. My reply to him was something like this: "Ed, it's great to hear from you. If I could go back and change what happened, I don't think I would, based on new choices I've made in my life."

Then it occurred to me that Ed might be hoping I'd forgive him for never being there. Doing so took some serious Grit, but it not only freed Ed, it freed me as well. The power to forgive someone in your life—a friend, a family member, a business associate—is a choice, and that power of choice can be transformative. As a

167

Christian, I thank God for giving me the strength to stand up to life's challenges, because that's when you learn. When you learn, you grow, and when you grow, you change. Change gives you an opportunity to reevaluate, reinvent and reignite your life, your passion and your drive. You can stand back up when you get knocked down.

Brendon McCarthy (right) and his family: (from left) his son Drew, wife Teresa and daughter Kelly.

Back when I was 19, I had no way of knowing that someday I would be using my story as a backdrop to inspire others, nor could I ever have imagined my dear friend Brendon McCarthy calling me religiously for the past 34 years on the day of my anniversary just to remind me of how far I have come.

From St. George Island, I drove to Bay Medical Community Hospital. It was a 1 ½-hour drive, and my mind was wandering. I thought a lot about what took place during my time there so many years ago. I thought about my sister, Heidi, and brother, Mark, how young they were seeing me for the very first time just days after my accident.

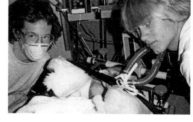

Heidi and Mark watching over me.

I was excited to see that Dr. Stringer, now in his mid-70s, was still practicing. I rolled into his office using my wheelchair, which I need today if I am traveling a distance. I finally came to terms with it.

"I'm sure you don't remember me," I told him, "but 22 years ago you saved my life. I want to thank you and show you how far I have come." At that moment, I stood up, walked over to him and shook his hand.

He had no idea that I was mobile. "You've come a long way," he said, clearly surprised. "What are you doing these days?"

I told him about my speaking and my desire to share my message with others. He agreed that I have so much to offer those willing to allow my experiences to inspire their own efforts through personal struggles. Dr. Stringer's confirmation brought tears to my eyes.

Looking back on the choices I had made since that night on St. George Island, I realized I had been given an opportunity to see the world from an entirely new perspective.

Today, at 53, I am amazed at how many lives my story has impacted. Life is about giving back, and I am trying as best as I can to do my part. Making a difference is something I believe everyone should strive for. First, you've got to believe you can—then *let it happen!*

This caricature was drawn live as I presented to Radio Flyer's Annual Sales Conference. It blew me away! Hope you enjoy it, too.

BROTHERLY LOVE

Some of us have siblings. In most cases, growing up they can
be a pain in the neck. It was that way with my brother, Mark,
and sister, Heidi, two people I love dearly. On November 3, 2007,
Mark sent me an email that moved me to tears. He wrote:

I remember the Sunday morning after your accident. It seems like yesterday. I was working at Turtle Creek Country Club when Dad showed up and told me you were in a car accident and the doctors were unsure if you would make it or not and, if you did, if you would ever walk again. Dad walked away toward his office and stayed there for hours.

When he came out of his office, he walked up to me and said "Your mother and I are going to leave for the hospital in Panama City, Florida, and I am not sure when we will return." He asked me to call around to all the relatives and tell them what had happened and said he would be in touch once he knew more.

After he left, sitting for an hour or so, crying most of the time, I found myself saying, "Why Scott and not me?" I never understood why I thought those thoughts. It's funny, but growing up, I always looked up to you and wanted to be just like you. I bet you didn't know that.

I'm not sure why I'm telling you this, but I've been thinking of you a lot this week. It is your anniversary, I suppose. I am very proud of you and what you've accomplished throughout your life. Keep it up, Bro. — *Love, Mark*

ACKNOWLEDGMENTS

I have nothing but praise for my family, as well as the coaches, mentors and literary professionals who have helped make this book a reality. A big thanks to the editor, Joy Margolis, Stand Up Incorporated's publisher, Mike Murray, and special contributors, Mark and Tom Burrows and Denise Weston, who were involved from beginning to end in the production of this book.

Thanks to Stand Up Incorporated and Pearhouse Press for ensuring this book benefits people in nations around the world. Finally, and most importantly, I extend a big heartfelt *thank you* to my mom, Joan Burrows, my dad, Tom Burrows, my stepmom, Susan, my brother, Mark, and his wife, Dawn, my sister, Heidi, and her husband, Eric, as well as the rest of my extended family, who have been my cheerleaders and encouragers every step of the way.

BIBLIOGRAPHY

Books

Adams, Christopher Robin. *Our Marrowed Souls*

Berg, Art. *Finding Peace in Troubled Waters*. Salt Lake City: Desert Books, 1998.

Berg, Art. *Some Miracles Take Time*. Highland, Utah: Invictus Press, 1998.

Berg, Art. *The Impossible Just Takes a Little Longer: Living with Purpose and Passion*. New York, Harper: 2002.

Daniels, Aubrey. *Bringing Out the Best in People*. New York: McGraw-Hill, 1999.

Henley, William Ernest. *Invictus*. London: Modern British Poetry, Louis Untermeyer Edition, 1920.

Kushner, Harold. *When Bad Things Happen To Good People*. New York: Anchor, 2004.

Laughlin, Chuck. *Samurai Selling*. New York: St. Martin's, 1994.

Peck, Scott. *The Road Less Traveled*. New York: Simon & Schuster, 1978.

Reeve, Christopher. *Still Me*. New York: Random House, 1998.

Siegel, Bernie. *Love, Medicine, and Miracles*. New York: HarperCollins, 1988.

Von Oeck, Roger. *A Whack on the Side of the Head*. New York: Warner Books, 1983.

Von Oeck, Roger. *A Kick in the Seat of the Pants*. New York: Perennial Library, 1986.

Wimbrow, Dale. *The Man in the Glass*. New York: 1934.

Periodical

Macauly, Cathie. "A Walking Tribute to Courage." Jensen Beach, Florida: *The Mirror*, 1985.

just want to put faces to some of the names I've mentioned in this book and share a few memorable experiences.

*My sister, **Heidi**. & her husband, Eric Shea*

*Karley, Kaitlyn, **Rick**, Renee & Cory Justice*

*Katelyn, **Hank**, Sabrina & Landon Dobbs*

*Loren & **Steve** Muro*

*Robin, Olivia, Courtney, Rachael & **Ronnie** Kirchman*

*TJ, Katie, Margarete & **Todd** Laycock*

*Skylar, Allen, **Sunni** & Alec Ashforth*

Mom and I at the Grand Ole Opry after I presented to MetLife. So proud to introduce her to 300 people.

Uncle Jim. Always there for me and everyone else. Known for one word that inspired us all: Tremendous.

Grateful to have such support from my *Aunt Terry, Uncle Don* and *Uncle Russ* (lower left).

Karen and Doug Greenwell. Doug is my cousin from Quincy, Illinois, who was instrumental in getting me to speak to my first insurance and financial client: Country Insurance and Financial Services.

On left, **Jim Wilson**, my Kung Fu karate instructor, aka Si-Fu.

Dee Dee Hicks, college classmate on St. George Island.

Charles Benoit (white hat) and **Scott Sears**. Fraternity brothers who saved my life by taking me to emergency care.

Michael and Sabre Duhart. He was my wide receiver teammate in high school and inspiration.

(left to right) **Aunt Diane**, my godmother, **Mom**, me and friend **Tom Beert**. Aunt Diane has always been there for me and others and is the hardest-working person I know.

(left to right) **Tristan, Victor, Justin, Nathan Simmons**. Victor, father of these three, was a defensive back in high school who challenged me daily to do better. Justin plays defensive back for the Denver Broncos.

(left to right) Me, **Marrenne Bradford, Kim, Bob Bradford.** *The Bradfords hosted a fundraising event to help my parents cover costs not covered by insurance. I'm most grateful.*

(left to right) Me and the boys, 30 years later. **John Salvador, Ronnie Kirchman, Brendon McCarthy, Todd Laycock, Me, Rick Justice.**

Me and **John Schmitt** *in Greece. I'm wearing his Super Bowl III Champion Ring. Two words engraved on it: POISE and EXECUTION.*

After hearing me speak, **Sue Lopez** *said, "When I climb Mount Kilimanjaro, I'm going to send you a picture of your book cover from the top to show others what can happen when you put your Vision, Mindset and Grit into action."*

*It was a privilege to speak to our troops at **Minot Air Force Base**. They are fighting for our freedom every day.*

*After I spoke at the Million Dollar Round Table Global Conference in Bangkok, **Kim** and I flew to Phuket, then took a boat ride to Pei Pei Island. "The Beach," starring Leonardo DiCaprio, was filmed there. Kim is a yoga instructor. Before we left, I caught her in this pose and took this breathtaking picture.*

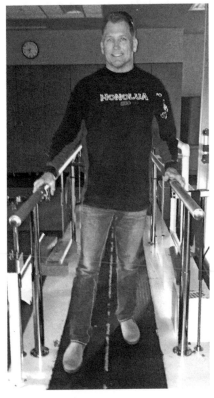

Returning to Craig Hospital 35 years later, I had a humbling experience standing in the same parallel bars.

Million Dollar Round Table Experience and Global Conference
Bangkok, Thailand - 9,000 Attendees

SCOTT BURROWS' message is one of HOPE and SUCCESS. He shows people how to turn adversity into opportunity.

Scott inspires, energizes and motivates people to change their thinking, turn setbacks into comebacks, achieve unprecedented results and accomplish their absolute best. While his presentations are specifically customized for your organization and its core values and objectives, his very personal story is delivered with thought-provoking life lessons and humorous anecdotes that involve the audience and touch each person deeply. Scott's principles of **VISION, MINDSET** and **GRIT** will have a profound impact on your attendees and your organization's culture long after the applause has ended.

To book Scott for your next event, email him at
scott@scottburrows.com
or visit his website:
www.scottburrows.com